Forever, Amen.

Forever, Amen.

Earl C. Davis

BROADMAN PRESS
Nashville, Tennessee

© Copyright 1982 • Broadman Press

All rights reserved.

4219-53

ISBN: 0-8054-1953-5

Dewey Decimal Classification: 226.96

Subject Heading: LORD'S PRAYER

Library of Congress Catalog Card Number: 81-67199

Printed in the United States of America

To
the glory of my Heavenly Father
and to
the memory of my earthly father,
Edward C. Davis
1914-1981

About the Author

Dr. Earl C. Davis is pastor of the First Baptist Church of Memphis, Tennessee. The church's ministry is multiplied since Dr. Davis preaches on radio and television every week.

He is active in denominational life, having served as a member of the SBC Committee on Committees, as president of the Georgia Baptist Pastors' Conference, and as a member of the Tennessee Baptist Convention's World Hunger Committee. He currently is a member of the Baptist World Alliance Commission on Pastoral Leadership and a member of the Trustees of the Baptist Sunday School Board.

He is a graduate of Stetson University (B.A.), Southeastern Baptist Theological Seminary (B.D.), and The Southern Baptist Theological Seminary (Ph.D). Before coming to Memphis he had pastored the Ekron Baptist Church, Ekron, Kentucky; the First Baptist Church, Marianna, Florida; and the First Baptist Church, Dalton, Georgia.

He speaks at state and nationwide Bible study and evangelism conferences and writes for a number of periodicals.

He and Mrs. Davis (Peggy) have two children, Deryl and Dawn.

CONTENTS

1
Does God Answer Prayer?

Matthew 26:36-45

According to statistics I have seen, practically everybody prays. Ninety-eight percent of all churched people pray. Seventy-six percent of those who do not have any church affiliation say they pray too! Eighty-seven percent of teenagers say they pray daily. Seventy percent of all those who pray say their prayers are answered. Sixty percent say that they could be said to live lives of constant prayer![1]

If we believe the statistics, everybody seems to pray. The rise in the number of prayer groups in our country is encouraging. There is a continuing and even mounting opposition to the decision of the Supreme Court which, for practical purposes, virtually outlawed prayer in the public schools. A recent front-page headline of the *Wall Street Journal* read like this: "Astonished homeowners have trouble selling. Some change tactics: Are trying prayer."

Not long ago I received a letter from a stranger:

DEAR PASTOR,

   I am very concerned about my daughter
and grandson. She left Panama City, Florida,
three weeks ago. She calls but won't tell of her
whereabouts. If you should learn anything of
their whereabouts, please let me know by mail.
I am praying.

   The basic question is, *Is* there anything
to prayer? Do all people pray? Do all people
pray alike? Does the unbeliever really pray?
Can he pray? Does God hear the prayer of
the unbeliever and the prayer of the believer
equally? Let us sketch a picture of that average nonchurched American first of all, and
then we'll sketch a picture of the churched
American.
   What kind of person is the unchurched
American? He's a good old boy. He's probably your brother-in-law. He is more interested in material things, in getting ahead in
this world, than he is in spiritual things and
the place of God in his life.
   Now, *when* does he pray? If I may be so
bold as to tell you about your brother-in-
law, I would say he prays primarily when in
trouble, when his back is to the wall. His attitude toward prayer may be much like the
attitude of the seaman who had just re-
turned from a voyage. To a query from another sailor about the voyage, he replied, "It

was a good voyage; there was only a call to prayer twice. On one of those occasions, there was no more need to pray than if suddenly you and I should fall down here on the pavement and raise our voices to God!"

Your brother-in-law probably divides life into copeable and uncopeable circumstances. That with which he can cope, he handles. That with which he cannot cope, that which is bigger than he, he attacks with prayer.

He also prays when he wants something. He seems to see prayer and God like a child sees a piggy bank that he turns upside down and shakes. Sometimes there's money in it and sometimes there isn't, but it doesn't hurt to shake it!

So often your brother-in-law is like the little fellow who entered a drugstore kicking and screaming, throwing a regular tantrum. The mother explained to the druggist that the tantrum was the result of her not buying a particular toy the child wanted. The druggist, in an effort to soothe both mother and child, said to the child, "Surely you don't pitch fits like this all the time. Does your mother buy you whatever you want when you pitch a fit like this?"

The child replied, "Well, sometimes she does and sometimes she don't, but it don't cost nothin' to pitch a fit!"

This concept of prayer is very foreign to the Christian view of prayer. The unbeliever does not see the kind of relationship that is inherent in prayer. Rather, he prays because there is a streak of superstition in him. His feelings are like that of Huck Finn:

Miss Watson she took me in the closet and prayed, but nothing come of it. She told me to pray every day, and whatever I asked for I would get it. But it warn't so. I tried it. Once I got a fishline, but no hooks. It warn't any good to me without hooks. I tried for the hooks three or four times, but somehow I couldn't make it work. By and by, one day, I asked Miss Watson to try for me, but she said I was a fool. She never told me why, and I couldn't make it out no way.

I set down one time back in the woods, and had a long think about it. I says to myself, if a body can get anything they pray for, why don't Deacon Winn get back the money he lost on pork? Why can't the widow get back her silver snuffbox that was stole? Why can't Miss Watson fat up? No, says I to myself, there ain't nothing in it.

I remember hearing of a Georgia boy who went to seminary in Kentucky. He became pastor of a church in the Bluegrass area. The first Sunday in the new church one of his members asked, in a very solemn way, if the congregation might have prayer for Lucy Gray. Well, the young pastor wanted to do everything he could to get off to a good start. If Lucy Gray needed prayer, he would see that she got prayer. Not only did he storm the bastions of heaven in public prayer for Lucy Gray, but he also asked the congregation to pray all week for Lucy Gray. The next Sunday he did the same thing.

On the third Sunday, the member who requested the prayer took his pastor aside and thanked him for his prayer support. He informed the pastor rather dejectedly that there was no more need to pray for Lucy Gray.

The young pastor's face fell and he was deeply disturbed, "Oh, my brother, I'm sorry to hear it. Did she die?"

"Oh no! She lost the race!"

So your brother-in-law prays when he's in trouble or when he wants something. He has, basically, a superstitious outlook about prayer. But the real clincher is that he has absolutely no intention of letting his prayers control his life. Prayer is a tool to get what he wants. He never intends to let his life get out of hand through the power of prayer.

Consider now what the New Testament tells us about prayer. Study the life of Jesus, his teachings, and his concepts of prayer and then turn to the early church and the practice of prayer and the apostle Paul. A great contrast can be seen between the Christian practice of prayer and the way your brother-in-law prays.

Three pictures may gather up the images of prayer in the New Testament for us. First, prayer can be characterized as two friends talking. Imagine a cold winter night, snow outside, a roaring fire, a comfortable chair, good company, and good conversation. That's one picture of the way prayer ought to be. It ought to be a sharing of hopes, fears, sorrows, and the day's events between the Christian and God. It ought to be worship, adoration, and quietness.

Your brother-in-law doesn't know what that means. He's never been able to practice or to see prayer that way. He may not even wish to. He will feel a bit more kinship with the second picture: A child going to his father for help. Often where there is serious illness, I will pray, "Lord, we desperately ask for this person to be healed. As a child comes to his father and asks for the desire of his heart, we pray that you will hear our prayer and answer our plea. But, Father, we know that your will is best and to that will we submit."

When we as Christians pray, we enter into the presence of God as a child who asks for something from his father and trusts that he will get an answer. I would never give my child a loaded gun as a toy, nor will God give his child a loaded gun. Now, my child may play in another yard and pick up a knife or a broken piece of glass and hurt himself. Just so, some of us wander into the devil's backyard and do the same thing.

The third picture of Christian prayer which contrasts so strongly with the way your brother-in-law prays is that of a soldier receiving orders from his commander. Part of prayer is standing in the presence of God to ask for the knowledge, the wisdom, the ability, the strength to stand against the devil and make each day count as a day for Christ.

The differences between the way your brother-in-law prays and Christian prayer can be illustrated with the story of Elijah and the priests of Baal (1 Kings 18). Elijah, being human, couldn't resist a little taunting. He told the false priests to offer their sacrifice first. "There are a lot of you; you ought to be able to dress that animal and throw him on the altar and call down fire in no time flat! You go first." They screamed; they chanted; they paraded around. They whooped; they yelled; but no fire fell from heaven to burn the sacrifice. Noontime approached. Elijah was sitting under the shade tree. He called out every now and then, "What's the matter? Is your god asleep? Has he gone on a trip? Is he out chasing somebody?" The priests of Baal only cried louder and cut themselves with rocks, stones, and knives.

Toward sunset Elijah poured buckets of water upon his altar and sacrifice and prepared to pray. In quietness, this man of God stood before the people and said, "Lord God, hear my prayer that these people may know that you are the living God, and I am thy servant." And the fire fell!

Do you see the contrast between the way unchurched Americans pray, with frenzy and desperation, and the way Christians pray in quietness, submitting to the will of God?

As I ponder this contrast, I see that it makes a great difference what we believe and how we go about praying. Some people have faith in prayer. That is, they believe that if one goes about it right and if one has the formula, then prayer will work. Such an approach borders on presumption. Some people have faith in prayer, and other people pray in faith. It is far more important to pray in faith, saying, "Father, thy will be done." We see that what people believe about God determines how they pray. Further, how people pray tells us a lot about what they believe about God.

So now, the question, Can an unbeliever really pray? No. The unbeliever can scream out in the night, but he cannot truly pray in the Christian sense of the word. For Christian prayer is the result of a relationship, and the unbeliever has no relationship from which his prayer life can flow.

Study now some of the amazing aspects of prayer. First, Christian prayer is *embarrassing*. Have you ever felt that? Christian prayer makes us uncomfortable; genuine, honest prayer often leads to a real sense of guilt. There is no way to honestly pray without our sins marching before us, legion upon legion, mocking us. All of our betrayals of Christ, all of our unforgiving attitudes toward others, all of our lack of witness march in front of us. They stick out their tongues and laugh at us when we bow down to pray. We cannot really pray if part of our lives are closed off from God. That's why prayer is uncomfortable, for it literally shatters this world. See the way Isaiah portrayed prayer when he spoke of that great vision of God (ch. 6). In prayer Isaiah's world fell away! There he stood before Almighty God. Suddenly Isaiah became painfully aware of being a man of unclean lips who dwelt in the midst of an unclean people.

Think of David. In his time of deepest sin, sorrow, and need, he fell on his face and said, "Against thee [God], thee only, have I sinned, and done this evil in thy sight." Though he had sinned against Uriah and others, he rightly surmised that his sins were basically against God. Then David said, "My sin is ever before me." So it is with Christian prayer. Simon Peter fell at the feet of Jesus when he realized who Jesus is and said, "Depart from me; for I am a sinful man, O Lord."

Secondly, Christian prayer will *purify the dominant desires of our hearts.* Christian prayer will purify those desires which run our lives. If the words of our prayers are not in tune with the deepest desires of our hearts, we are not really praying. Jesus, in the garden, prayed, "Father, . . . take away this cup from me." That was his deepest desire, you see, for his own self. But then in keeping with God's will he said, "Nevertheless, not what I will, but what thou wilt."

When we kneel to pray, the dominant desires of our hearts have to be brought closer to God's will if we are going to pray rightly. This was the problem with the Pharisees. They prayed as they thought they ought, but they didn't pray sincerely. What they said was not what they really wanted deep in their hearts. How refreshing Augustine was when he prayed, "Lord, make me pure," but then did have enough Christian conviction and honesty to say, "But not just yet, Lord!" That was because to be made pure was not the deepest desire of his heart at that time of his life.

So I ask you this question. Is it really prayer if we pray, "Lord, please feed those starving people in Thailand and Cambodia and around the world . . ." and then rise up from prayer and go to the nearest grocery store to find that new diet brand of puppy food because our puppy is getting too fat? Is that really prayer? Unless we do all we can to put legs on the prayer, is it really prayer? Should the prayer have been, "Lord, do what you can for the starving people, but first, would you take care of my puppy?" Wouldn't that have been prayer in a better sense of the word? Is it prayer if we say, "Lord, help me to be a better Christian," but we do not attend church, we do not tithe, we do not take part in the activities of our church? Is it really prayer when we say, "Lord, save the heathen," but we do not witness?

When most Christians kneel to pray, we have to begin by saying, "Lord, I want to desire your will. I'm willing for you to change me so I will want the right things."

A third aspect of Christian prayer is that

it *creates an entirely new situation.* When I
rise from morning prayer, when I finish a
prayer by the bedside of someone who's
deathly ill, when at the funeral I pray for the
family, a new situation is born. I really believe that when we say, "Amen" things are
different. For we have asked our Father to
take charge of the situation. When I was a
child and got into trouble or needed help, all
I had to do was ask my father. After asking
for help, I felt different about my problem. I
knew that the situation had changed. I had
put it in his hands.

We cannot overlook the fact that Christian prayer is shaped and given substance
by the silences. It is not true Christian prayer
to rush into the presence of God and blurt
out our demands and then run out again.
That's not conversation and that's not
prayer.

Christian prayer *has some limitations.*
Christian prayer is limited by our sins. How
we have overemphasized and misinter-
preted this verse, "If ye have faith as a grain
of mustard seed, . . . nothing shall be impossible unto you." He who said that also
taught us to pray, "Forgive us as we forgive
those who have committed transgressions
against us!" (Matt. 6:12, *author's paraphrase).* We ask God to forgive us only to the
extent that we forgive others. Therefore, my

sins limit the power of prayer. As a father who desires the best for his children, God can't do just anything I want him to do. Our prayers are limited further by the formula with which we close our Christian prayers: In Jesus' name. When we close a prayer in Jesus' name, we are saying, "Lord, I believe that what I am praying is in the spirit, character, and will of Jesus." I fear a realization of that truth would often make us tongue-tied before God.

Christian prayer *changes people and things*. Adoniram Judson said, "I never sincerely and earnestly prayed for anything but that someday, no matter how distant, how far off, yet it was answered; that somehow and often in the form that I would least expect, it was answered." He prayed "Lord, let me go to India as a missionary," yet he ended up in Burma. He prayed earnestly, "Lord, heal my wife," yet he buried his wife and both his children. He prayed earnestly, "Lord, don't let me go to prison," yet he was there for months. All of his prayers were, indeed, answered, but not in his way. They were answered beyond his way.

A fellow pastor pondered the account of Jesus and his disciples in Gethsemane. Jesus prayed through the dark night for the Father's will. When the cross was the answer, he went to die in peace. His disciples were told to pray for strength, yet they slept through the night. Dawn came, and the Savior was composed while the disciples fled in confusion. If they had prayed as Jesus prayed, if they had stayed awake and watched with him, would they, like him, have been strengthened by the angels? Would they, like him, have gone quietly to their crosses with him? Perhaps so. Sometimes our lack of prayer keeps us from being the kind of people God wants us to be, from sharing the kind of sorrows that God wants us to share.

I like the story Nathanael Hawthorne tells of the little boy who gazed at the great stone face on the mountain so much that it became mirrored in his own face and life.

An unknown poet of sensitive heart wrote:

> Every morning lean thine arms awhile
> Upon the window-sill of heaven
> And gaze upon thy Lord,
> Then, with the vision in thy heart,
> Turn strong to meet the day.

Note

1. *Emerging Trends.* Vol. I, no. 10, December, 1979.

2
The Meaning of "Our Father"

Matthew 5:43-48

Our Father who art in heaven, Hallowed be thy name. Thy kingdom come, Thy will be done, On earth as it is in heaven. Give us this day our daily bread; And forgive us our debts, As we also have forgiven our debtors; And lead us not into temptation, But deliver us from evil (Matt. 6:9-13, RSV).

Not long ago a magazine article dealing with prayer stated that prayer is simply talking to one's self. Is prayer merely a device by which we gain our inner composure and sort out our thoughts? Must we accept the idea that prayer is only a vestige of the "dark forest syndrome"—a reflex we feel in the stress, tension, and strain of our times; harking back to a dim past in which people, wandering in a lonesome world felt that even the lightning, the storm, and the darkness seemed always against them? Do we, like our ancestors, feel like children lost in a dark forest yearning desperately for somebody to come along and say, "Here, child, take my hand and I will show you the way out of the forest"?

Needless to say, I do not agree with that definition of prayer or that assessment of the power of prayer. Let us not waste time seeking to demonstrate the validity of prayer. An unanswerable argument for prayer lies close at hand: All people pray! Whatever else we would say about prayer, however we feel about it, there is no escape from the basic fact that all people pray. No matter who the person is, no matter how self-important, no matter whether he feels he can live without God, his neighbor, the church, the Bible, or the blood of Christ, in his hour of need and crisis, every person will lift up his voice to some power greater than himself. He may not call this power God, but for him it is.

The question is, How shall we pray? The disciples came to Jesus saying, "Master, how shall we pray?" They had observed the power of Jesus raising the dead, casting out devils, and forbidding the demons to speak. But when the disciples wanted such power, their plea was not, "Master, teach us how to cast out demons. Master, teach us how to raise the dead. Master, teach us how to straighten crippled arms." But knowing that the mainspring of his life was prayer, knowing that the strength of his life was communion with his Father, they came to him and said, "Lord, teach us to pray" (Luke 11:1).

He taught them to pray. "Pray then like this: Our Father who art in heaven, Hallowed be thy name. Thy kingdom come, Thy will be done, On earth as it is in heaven. Give us this day our daily bread; And forgive us our debts, [strangely enough he linked them together] As we also have forgiven our debtors; And lead us not into temptation, But deliver us from evil. For thine is the kingdom, and the power, and the glory, for ever. Amen" (Matt. 6:9-13a, RSV; 13b, KJV).

The Lord's Prayer is very short, so brief that it is comfortable with the smallness of our world. A smallness characterized by the common sight of the Lord's Prayer—or even the whole Sermon on the Mount—inscribed on a microdot. Yet, it is also true that the depth, the richness, the power of the Lord's Prayer is such that only creation in its entirety can hold it.

Despite its brevity, the Lord's Prayer is not to be used as a charm, a talisman. When we look carefully at the Lord's Prayer we find that it is not a soft, saccharine pill to soothe us in this world of woe. Rather, this prayer consists of brief statements of strong theology; an outline of Christian commitment, Christian faith, Christian theology.

Let's look at the very first phrase, "Our Father who art in heaven." How can we pray that? If I pray, "Our Father who art in heaven," I am saying that the nature of God is like a father. That does not mean God is like my father or like your father. This affirmation is not based upon my father or upon my own fatherhood.

Jesus said we should look at God like this. Jesus, not you and me, said, "Our Father, which art in heaven." Therefore, the Father of which Jesus spoke is greater and larger and more eternal than any father we've ever know. The Father of whom Jesus spoke is our model for the character we are to live out, loving and caring and giving. The teaching that God is Father is unique to Jesus.

No religious leader before Jesus saw God as a personal father. The pagans referred to their god as "father Zeus" and "father Jupiter," but that was only in a vague, broad, nationalistic way. In the Old Testament, we read, "father Abraham" and "father God" even, in some sense as father of a nation. Men like Hosea glimpsed every now and then that God, like a father, had led his people out of Egypt. But it was a nation that Hosea glimpsed God leading with tenderness like a father.

It remained for Jesus of Nazareth to

teach us that God is a *personal* father to you and to me. It remained for Jesus to emphasize that not merely a "great" saint here and there can reach up and claim that understanding, but all frail, feeble, sinful "lesser" saints can lift their eyes to heaven and declare, "Thou art my Father."

Jesus drew his picture of God as Father from the background of Jewish fatherhood. In the background is gray-headed, white-bearded Jacob laying his hands upon his children and blessing them. In the corners of Jesus' picture of God as Father is the Jewish father who remembers the words of the Old Testament, who fastens them upon his forehead and upon his wrists, who remembers the admonition to teach the way of God to his children when he walks in the way, when he sits at the meal, and when he lies down at night. In the background of Jesus' teaching is the Jewish father who goes up to Jerusalem faithfully to keep the religious feasts, the Jewish father who keeps the religious laws, the father of the prodigal son. God is Father like that father, who will put a lamp in the window, who will watch day after day, and night after night, until the child who has overstepped his boundaries finally comes limping home again. God is like that.

That is what Jesus was saying when he

said God is like a father. The picture which
Jesus painted and lifted up beyond all mor-
tal models and understanding is a picture of
a father of love, kindness, authority, concern, and integrity. I suppose nothing trou-
bled Jesus more than the lack of understanding God as Father. In Jesus' prayer in
Gethsemane, he said, "Father, they never
knew you. They never understood that you
are a father. But, I understand and those
whom you have given me, my disciples,
they understand" (see John 17). Paul took
this great truth and planted it squarely in the
middle of Christian theology when he said
that, upon our conversion, we are given the
spirit of kinship by which we cry out,
"Abba, Father!" Jesus taught us to say,
"Abba." That word is not to be translated
stiffly as "father," but rather translates as
"papa" or "daddy." Jesus said God is like
that.

But is God really like that? Can beaten-
down people on the street believe God is
like that? Why should they believe God is
like that? Perhaps the longing for such a
father is merely *my* crying out in a dark forest. True, we do not see this character of
God from the world. I see cruelty, loneliness, unkindness, unconcern, hostility,
prejudice. What makes me think that God is
a father? Just because Jesus said it?

Here we see how important it is that Jesus taught people to pray, "Our Father which art in heaven." The only way I can believe there will be somebody who answers when I cry out in the forest is if there is a *miracle*.

If, by some chance, I have been told God's going to answer; if, by some miracle, he has called out to me first, then when I call out in the midst of the dark forest, I know I am not just screaming in the dark.

The Bible paints the coming of Jesus against just such a dark night: A forest of alienation, loneliness, anxiety, unforgiveness, a world of suffering and tormenting in which people cry out and say, "God, why is it like this?" The Bible says, "My child, it is like this, not because God wants it this way, but *because people have made it this way.*"

Life is like a dark forest because people in their rebellious hearts have cut themselves off from God. In so doing, people have cut themselves off from their neighbors. We have become children wandering in the dark forest of loneliness and unforgiveness.

In the midst of the dark forest, *a miracle happened*. God sent Jesus of Nazareth, both man and God, in whom God and his splendor can be seen. He sent Jesus to live, to die, to rise again, to say to people, "God is your Father. He loves you. Take his hand. He calls out to you in the midst of the forest." So you see, long before I was born or you were born, God was calling out in Christ.

You see, we've turned it around. We're saying, "If I cry out in the dark, is anybody going to hear?" The Bible tells us God has been calling out to us from the darkness, saying, "Look, here is my hand, grasp it." He has been calling out to us in Christ long before we even thought to cry out to him.

Since God has called out to us in Jesus Christ; since in him we hear God saying, "I am your Father. You are my child," light is shed upon many of the darkest areas of our lives. Look at the introduction to the account of the Lord's Prayer. "Be not ye therefore like [the hypocrites]: for your Father knoweth what things ye have need of, before ye ask him" (KJV). Did you understand that? He knows what we need before we even ask. Surely he does because he was here before we were. Before our small lives ever saw the light of day, God was before us, God was in Christ, calling out to us. He knows what we need before we need it, and he knows what we need when we do not even know.

Often, imprisoned behind bars we have forged of our own selfishness and rebellion, we cry out to God not for freedom but

for a Persian rug to put in the cell of our loneliness! Often when spiritually naked, we cry
out not for the clothes of righteousness but
for finger sandwiches to eat while we sit on
the curb! You see, we do not know how we
ought to pray. Therefore, how wonderful it
is that God was before us. He knows ahead
of time what we need. He even knows, contrary to what we ask, what we need.

Since I know that God is my Father, the
fact that he does not answer my prayers just
as I want them answered does not mean
that God is deaf or indifferent or hostile. It
means that God, knowing more than his ail-
ing child, is shaping a more beautiful, different, effective remedy for that which ails me.

Since God is my Father, light is shed on
another dark area of life, the realm of suffering. Since God is my Father, I can cry out to
him in the midst of my suffering, "Abba,
Father, take this from me!" I know that since
I cry to him in earnestness, whether he takes
this from me, he is going to fashion that
which is best for me as his child.

Jesus in the garden of Gethsemane cried
out, "Abba, Father, all things are possible
unto thee; take away this cup from me."
God did not take it from him. But he fashioned from that cross a thing which glows
through the centuries and leads people to
their eternal home.

There's another side of this coin. Since I pray to God as Father, does it not logically follow that God expects *obedience* and *fellowship*? Has God not the right to ask of me, if I am his child and he is my Father, to obey him? And, therefore, do I not have to ask myself if I am living by the light which has been brought to me in Jesus of Nazareth? Must I not say, Do I love this Book which is his revelation of his will for me? Is it one of my cherished possessions? Must I not ask myself about my relationship to the church for which Christ died? Must I not ask myself, Am I coming as often as a child ought to come to his Father, kneeling for communion with my Father?

If I am his child, then he can expect from me obedience to his will and a fellowship with him. But that is not all. If I'm going to call God Father, then I'm claiming a kinship. He has a right to expect that kinship to show.

My older brother is the "spittin' image," as people used to say, of our maternal grandfather. "My stars," people would comment, "if James Davis doesn't look just like old Jim Seago, I never saw such." Don, my brother immediately younger than me, had red hair and blue eyes as a child. Folk would say, "Yes, anybody can tell in a minute that you are 'Red' Davis's boy."

Doesn't God have the right to expect us to be the "spittin' image" of him.

The very first word of the Lord's Prayer, *our*, fractures the hermit life. A little poem says it beautifully:

> You cannot pray the Lord's Prayer
> In first person, "I"—
> You cannot say the Lord's Prayer
> And even once say "My."
> Nor can you pray the Lord's Prayer
> And not pray for another,
> For as you ask for "daily bread,"
> You must include your brother.
> Yes, others are included
> In each and every plea;
> From the beginning to the end of it,
> It doesn't once say "Me."
>
> *Author Unknown*

Me and *my* are not part of the Lord's Prayer. It says *us, ours,* and *we.* To pray this first phrase, "Our Father," is to recognize that God's love and concern is not mine exclusively. God's intention is not simply to draw to him numbers of separate people but to create a new community, fashioned in the image of the Father as seen in his Son, Jesus. Therefore, we must claim kinship with all God's children, realizing that everyone who claims Jesus as Savior is part of our family, regardless of color or social standing. We must welcome others gladly to worship with us. To say "Our Father," is either the crassest mockery or it is one of the deepest expressions of Christian fellowship that a person can utter.

To say "Our Father" means that we cannot come to the Lord's house and worship in solitude and separation. It means that we are aware when God's children are not gathered together, and we miss them. If we are God's children, we must have our Father's concern for all his children. Here is a mandate for the extension of Christianity. We cannot be elder siblings and forget about the prodigal.

"Our Father, which art in heaven"—only six words—but the other words in the prayer are only commentary upon them.

3
The Intention of Heaven

Revelation 22:1-5

Our Father *who art in heaven,* Hallowed be thy name. Thy kingdom come, Thy will be done, On earth as it is in heaven. Give us this day our daily bread; And forgive us our debts, As we also have forgiven our debtors; And lead us not into temptation, But deliver us from evil (Matt. 6:9-13, RSV).

When Jesus taught his disciples to pray, he first directed their attention (and ours) toward heaven. "Our Father *who art in heaven . . . .*" There are many reasons Jesus pointed his disciples to heaven, and we shall examine some of them in a moment, but first let us reflect on the importance of the reality of heaven in our lives as Christians.

In these closing years of the twentieth century, much interest has developed in the life beyond. Much of the orientation is neither Christian nor biblically based, but springs from the disillusionment and insecurity of this present world. It is, however, uniquely the Christian's privilege and joy to meditate upon the glories of heaven. As children of the Heavenly Father, you and I certainly need to know all we can about our Father's dwelling place and our future home.

To turn our hearts toward heaven gives Christians great encouragement. Some of the most powerful words uttered at gravesides gain strength because they look forward to our resurrection and eternal life in the Father's house: "Therefore, my beloved brethren, be ye stedfast, unmoveable, always abounding in the work of the Lord, forasmuch as ye know that your labour is not in vain in the Lord" (1 Cor. 15:58). Likewise Paul encouraged the church at Thessalonica to take heart in the inexorable and glorious approach of the world to come: "Then we which are alive and remain shall be caught up together with them in the clouds, to meet the Lord in the air: and so shall we ever be with the Lord. Wherefore comfort one another with these words" (1 Thess. 4:17-18).

Do you remember the beautiful scene in *The Pilgrim's Progress* when Christian and Hopeful approached the end of their journey and met the shepherds? These gentle folk dwelt in the edge of Emmanuel's Land and joyfully gave the travelers a view of the celestial city through their spyglass. The result was fresh desire to press on to the city.

Not only does our meditation upon heaven encourage us on our journey but it also gives us a needed perspective and understanding. Somewhere C. S. Lewis observed that the world is merely a great sculptor's shop. We are all statues—and there's a rumor going about that some of us are to come alive someday! The reality of heaven helps us see this life for what it is: the pale shadow of what God intended and what he will one day bring to pass. The poets have often said that we ought not call death a dreadful sleep, but rather call life on earth the sleep. Perhaps we awake in death to look back upon the dream called life. So Shelley spoke of Keats:

Peace, peace! he is not dead,
                    he doth/not sleep—
He hath awakened from the dream/of life.

The writer of Revelation most certainly stressed the reality of heaven and bid the beleaquered Christians to whom he wrote take fresh courage. Notice how chapters 2 and 3 of Revelation describe the struggle on a this-world level, as do the grim pictures of chapter 6. But chapters 4 and 5 describe a world more real than this world, existing

unseen alongside and above this sorry
scheme of things. It is a more real world in
which God dwells, in which there is peace,
joy, order, and rightness; a more real world
in which you and I as children of the Father
will one day dwell.

As we look at heaven through the windows of the Bible, I know that it is important
to us because every person has had a father
or mother, brother or sister, child or relative
to die. We want to think they dwell in
heaven, and we all want to think we will go
to heaven.

Someone spoke a deep truth wrapped
in humor when he said, speaking of three
surprises we will find in heaven: We will be
surprised to see some folk there we didn't
expect to see; surprised to note the absence
of some folk we did expect to see there; and
surprised to find that we ourselves are there!
I realize not all of us are going to heaven
and that heaven is uniquely the home of the
Christian.

Turning to the Bible to examine the
teaching on this topic, we find that para-
doxically the Book says both a little and a
lot. It speaks with a fine reserve, combining
negative definition with positive promises.

Why didn't Jesus say more in a concrete
way about heaven? Especially in light of his
underlining it in this Model Prayer? We must

keep in mind that we as humans—and the
Word became flesh—have no vocabulary,
no categories of speech in which to describe so different a life. It is as if I tried to describe a sunset to a man blind from birth; I
cannot speak sensibly of the overwhelm-
ing impression of evening shades of melted
gold, colors of the soft rose petal, or the
bluish tones slowly and majestically turning to deep purple, forming a cloak for the
night.

Perhaps, however, I could tell the blind
man that sunset is like a soft, soothing lullaby, and that sunrise is like a sturdy, robust
burst of music. That might give some help
to the blind man, but how do I describe the
difference between Brahms' *Lullaby* and
Tchaikovsky's *1812 Overture* to a totally
deaf man? Well, Tchaikovsky is like a sunrise, sturdy, confident, excited . . .

It may well be that if we had full knowledge of the glories of the Father's house we
would be intolerant of the limitations of
earth. To have that vision fully revealed to
our eyes, that glory ringing in our hearts,
might make us totally impatient with this
world. If a man had always lived deep in a
cave with only a candle for light and had
never seen the sunlight or ventured outside
the cave, rumors of a bright world where
men need not always carry their candle

would seem as an old wives' tale and receive the ridicule it deserved. But if the man
ever once went to the mouth of the cave and
saw that bright world outside . . .

Perhaps this is the point of the legends
which grew up surrounding the raising of
Lazarus from the grave. It was said he never
smiled again as long as he lived. Part of
Jesus' heaviness of heart at Lazarus' tomb
possibly sprang from the knowledge that
he was, in a sense, reshackling and recag-
ing this one, who ought not have to

> come back again to labor
> come back again to suffer
> where the famine and the fever
> wear the heart and waste the body.
>
> —*Author Unknown*

Poor Lazarus—back to the cage of earth,
to the dirty little village, to the daily round, to
days of dreaming, longing, waiting for the
glories he had tasted in the Father's house.

So it is surely in the wisdom of the Father
that the Bible has a gentle hesitation about
heaven. Yet it lays before us many encouraging hints of that distant glory. As we now
gather up those hints to shape them into a
meaningful shadow of that world, we shall
first deal with the basic question about
heaven, Why have heaven anyway?

What is God's intention in creating

heaven? A study and comparison of Genesis 3 and Revelation 22:1-5 will reveal that heaven is the full and complete expression of God's will for humanity. In Genesis 3, we are shown vividly the rebellion of humanity, our desertion of God's sovereignty and our dependence upon self, as Adam violates the tree of good and evil. As the Genesis tragedy unfolds, we see a scene of loneliness: a seeking God and a guilty pair, an empty, dark Garden. Shut out and under the curse, humanity stares back from exile at the Garden gate and its angel sentinel. This is a description not of God's will for people, but of people's arrogant and abortive will for themselves. The rest of the Bible is the story of God's search for people, God's invitation to come to a garden fairer than Eden, where all the intentions of the Father which were overturned in Eden shall be set right again, and people shall walk again in the evening with God.

Revelation 22:1-5 is a picture of the fulfilled intention of God for humanity. God is sovereign upon the throne of the universe; there is no night, no more curse, no more separation, no more loneliness. The second garden is the fullness of the intention of God.

Heaven is God's no to this world's sin, suffering, and death. Heaven is God's rejection of the world's rejection! Heaven is God's yes to his original intention to create people for fellowship with him.

It is important for us to realize that heaven is not merely a continuation of our fleshly, rebellious lives on a sensuous and never-ending level; nor is heaven the other extreme of the spiritualist in which we are absorbed into the "Divine Spirit" with no individual experience. Rather, heaven is an act of redemption. It is the redemption of our corruptible bodies, the renewal of our natures and our bodies, and the restoration of the fellowship we lost in Eden.

While heaven is a retrieval of what our rebellion and self-love has taken, it is much more. There is so much more than merely gaining back the ground lost. Vacationing some years back, my twelve-year-old son hooked a tarpon off the Florida coast. Back and forth the battle raged, first the boy yelling for help, then the reel screaming as the tarpon stripped more line. The guide had attached a red marker on the fishing line to help us fish at a particular depth. As boy and fish battled, sometimes the marker would be resurrected from the depth when the boy cranked line in. A cheer would go up from the fellow fishermen. But his delight at recovering the lost ground—soon to be lost again with a fresh surfacing and diving of the fish—was nothing in comparison to his joy when he possessed the fish on dry land! So heaven is much more than a recovery of what sin has taken away. It is the experience of the highest, fullest, ultimate expression of God's glorious will for you and me.

The glories of life in the Father's house arc the deepest expression of the Father's love, encompassing as it does the sacrificial death of the Father's Son to bring heaven within our grasp. Who can read of that great multitude around God's throne in Revelation 7—those who have washed their robes and made them white in the blood of the Lamb—and not remember the words of the prophet in Isaiah 53:11: "He shall see of the travail of his soul, and shall be satisfied." When the trumpet shall sound and time shall be no more, then it shall be known throughout heaven and earth that the Suffering Servant, the Lion of Judah, the Lamb of God, the King of kings has triumphed! He shall see the fruit of his agony, the great multitude of recreated men and women, boys and girls. It will be worth it— worth the incarnation, the pain, the sorrow, the rejection, and the death!

The intention of heaven is the full expression of the Father's love. When all is done, throughout eternity the wondering words of the angels as they gaze upon the stable, the cross, the grave, the blood-washed multitude will be: See how he loved them!

From the intention of the Father in creating heaven, let us turn our thoughts to the chief joy of heaven. Have you ever speculated as to what aspect of heaven's glories will provide the greatest joy? Have you assumed your greatest joy will be to ''walk the golden streets,'' greet loved ones now departed, or to talk with the great men of faith like Moses, Abraham, or Paul? If we study carefully the hints of heaven in the Bible, we will realize that the *presence of God* will bring the greatest joy even heaven can afford.

In each of the three pictures of heaven in Revelation 21 and 22—the visions of the tabernacle, the city, and the garden—God is at the center. In the scenes of heaven in Revelation 4 and 5, either the Father or the Son is the focus. In Revelation 7, the blood-washed throng is not the focus, for they gather around the throne of God. In John 14 we are promised by Jesus, in his comments on heaven, that *where he is* we shall find our place.

The presence of God will give meaning to all the other joys of heaven, just as the absence of God is the essence of hell. Perhaps we must admit that for most of us, the joy of reunion in heaven is uppermost, yet we can take comfort realizing that the Father knows we see through a glass, darkly, in this world.

4
Exploring the Father's House

John 14:1-6

Our Father *who art in heaven,* Hallowed be thy name. Thy kingdom come, Thy will be done, On earth as it is in heaven. Give us this day our daily bread; And forgive us our debts, As we also have forgiven our debtors; And lead us not into temptation, But deliver us from evil (Matt. 6:9-13, RSV).

Somewhere I read about a conversation F.W.H. Meyers, a British churchman, had with a woman whose daughter had recently died. Upon his inquiry about the state of the daughter's soul, the mother replied: "Oh, well, I suppose she is enjoying eternal bliss, but I wish you wouldn't talk about such unpleasant subjects." For some folk, the mention of our heavenly home is a dismal and painful subject. Small wonder that one of the perennial problems of prayer is unreality. If the glories of heaven are not meaningful and real to us in this dusty arena of every day, how can we pray with much meaning to the Father *"who art in heaven"*?

Yet we must confess that some of the simplest and most concrete questions about heaven leave us puzzled. Is heaven a place? It is a place and much more. Heaven is first and foremost a state of character unreachable in this life, then it is a place. To be in heaven is to be sinless, deathless, and in the presence of God. A careful study of the New Testament references to heaven will convince one of the priority of these aspects of character in the biblical view. But heaven is more than some*thing*, it is some*where*; it is a place. In John 14 we see both of these aspects of heaven stressed. Speculation concerning the whereabouts of heaven as a place is both commonplace and unfruitful. Even modern scientific curiosity is puny against the backdrop of God's universe, whose fringes only have been revealed. Some theologians feel that the renewed earth will be the heavenly home, basing this view on Romans 8 and Revelation 21. Perhaps the most we need to affirm is the reality of heaven as a place.

Will we have bodies? Yes, every indication from the Scriptures and common sense is that in heaven we will have bodies. We recall that Jesus had a postresurrection body. Moses and Elijah had bodies after death as they met with Jesus on the mount of trans-

figuration. Paul's distress in 2 Corinthians
5:1-4 seems to reveal a horror of giving up
this earthly body and experiencing the "in-
termediate state" between death and the
resurrection at the end of the world. He gave
a very positive word concerning the hope of
a body suitable for life in the Father's house.

The Christian's body in heaven will be a
fitting one, though apparently not a body of
flesh as we now experience. With gratitude,
we can be assured that in the perfection of
heaven there will be no mutilated, crippled,
wasted-away bodies. All these things will
have passed away. First Corinthians 15 emphasizes a connection between the body of
these days and the body of eternity, but it is
a connection such as the oak has to the
acorn, the butterfly to the caterpillar, the
Easter lily to the bulb.

Will there be degrees of reward? This
question of rewards is uppermost in many
people's mind. Yet I doubt it will be important when we finally reach heaven's
shores! If there are to be any differences of
reward, perhaps the key lies in the capacity
to enjoy heaven. A country preacher illustrated this point by saying that just as a hot,
tired plowman can drink more ice water at
the close of a hot day than can a man who
has spent the day in an air-conditioned office, so the depth of enjoyment of heaven

may be the answer to the question of degrees of reward.

Perhaps more helpful than random questions is the observation of heaven under a theme, such as *continuation.* There are some aspects, some characteristics and activities, of this life which will carry over into the next life.

There will be a continuation of our lives and personalities. Life goes on beyond the grave; of this the New Testament has no doubt. The old bit of doggerel may be true about Rover, but not about people:

> I had an old dog named Rover,
> When he died, he died all over.

As one man said, "Smashing the organ is not equivalent to killing the organist!" Our lives are not broken in two by death. We will be the same people, with the same personalities—cleansed, purified, matured.

Heaven is a place of continued *growth* and *achievement.* Evidently a perfect state does not prohibit growth. Although our Lord was without sin and lived a perfect life, we are told in the Gospels that he grew in knowledge and grace and in favor with God and people. Surely, then, we who are to become like Jesus will continue to grow and develop spiritually.

Heaven is a place of continued *work*

and *worship*. Rest is, of course, part of heaven. But inactivity and boredom are not part of the biblical picture of heaven. There will no doubt be tasks to perform, new challenges, time and opportunity to do the kind of things we never had the ability or time to accomplish here.

This particular realization of the joy of heaven hit me in a deeply moving way a few years ago. My family was riding down a quiet suburban road when my little daughter suddenly spied a beautiful little dollhouse in a backyard. It was an exact replica of the home in front. "I wish," said my daughter, "that I had a dollhouse like that." Only a father who feels that he has neglected his children to care for his church can fully recognize my feelings at that moment. Something deep inside me said, *Heaven is a place where fathers find time to build dollhouses they never built on earth.* I later built a slightly wacky dollhouse for Dawn. Heaven will, I think, provide the chance to do the good and noble and challenging things crowded out here on earth. Rudyard Kipling put it well:

> When Earth's last picture is painted,
>   and the tubes are twisted and dried,
> When the oldest colors have faded,
>   and the youngest critic has died,
> We shall rest, and, faith, we shall need it—

lie down for an aeon or two,
Till the Master of All Good Workmen
shall put us to work anew.

And those that were good shall be happy:
they shall sit in a golden chair;
They shall splash at a ten-league canvas
with brushes of comets' hair;
They shall find real saints to draw from—
Magdalene, Peter, and Paul;
They shall work for an age at a sitting,
and never be tired at all!

And only the Master shall praise us,
and only the Master shall blame;
And no one shall work for money,
and no one shall work for fame;
But each for the joy of the working,
and each, in his separate star,
Shall draw the Thing as he sees It
for the God of things as They Are!

As surely as work is a part of heaven, so will worship be. Here on earth there should be a rhythm of work and worship, and the same need is seen in heaven. The Book of Revelation heavily emphasizes the aspect of worship in heaven. In chapter 4 the four living creatures symbolizing all creation worship God day and night. Likewise the twenty-four elders who evidently represent God's people of the old and new covenants cast their crowns before the throne saying, "Thou art worthy, O Lord, to receive glory

and honour and power: for thou hast created all things, and for thy pleasure they are
and were created'' (Rev. 4:11).

As the Lamb comes upon the stage in
Revelation 5 and takes the book from the
hand of God, we see all creation lifting
voices in praise:

Saying with a loud voice, Worthy is the Lamb
that was slain, to receive power and riches and
wisdom, and strength, and honour, and glory,
and blessing. And every creature which is in
heaven, and on the earth, and under the earth,
and such as are in the sea, and all that are in
them, heard I saying, Blessing, and honour,
and glory, and power, be unto him that sitteth
upon the throne, and unto the Lamb for ever
and ever. And the four beasts said, Amen. And
the four and twenty elders fell down and wor-
shipped him that liveth for ever and ever (Rev.
5:12-14).

It is surely significant that there are more
hymns of worship in the Book of Revelation
than in any other book of the Bible except
Psalms. We often joke about how uncomfortable the folk who shun church on earth
will be in heaven, yet how true it is! The form
of worship will be different from our experience here, but the focus of heaven is our
adoration of and fellowship with God.

The theme of *knowledge* is important
as we think about our Father's house. There

is a torrent of questions about what we will *know* in heaven. Will we know each other? Will we be sad over friends who are not there? Do those already in heaven know about us? Will we know why certain things happened on earth; will we have full understanding?

The wise, old farmer's statement is a worthy starting point, "Surely we won't be bigger fools there than here!" There is no basis for blank minds in heaven; it is a place and a state of more knowledge, not less. "Then shall I know even also as I am known" (1 Cor. 13:12).

Surely we shall know each other in heaven. The eternal hope of grieving humanity through the ages has been that we shall know our loved ones and be known on the other side. This seems to be a God-implanted longing, and it is incredible that we should forget our dearest and closest when we experience God's greatest gift, heaven. It is unthinkable that we should not recognize and have fellowship with those with whom we sought and found eternal life, those with whom we made the pilgrimage to the celestial city.

In 1 Thessalonians, Paul comforted the Christians with the knowledge that Christ will bring our loved ones with him when he comes again, and mutual recognition is implied. When Jesus responded to the story of the seven brothers and one wife in Mark 12:20-25, he did not say they would not know each other in the world to come. He merely taught there will not be the earthly marriage relationship. Jesus taught and spoke as if we will know each other in heaven. He spoke of going to prepare a place for his disciples and then coming back to receive them "that where I am you may be also" (John 14:3, RSV).

A related concern of many Christians is whether we shall recognize great saints of generations gone by. This question opens the larger matter of fellowship with all the redeemed of all the ages. One of my favorite biblical scenes is Luke's account of the Last Supper. To this pathetic and untrustworthy band, Jesus promised a kingdom and declared they had stood with him through good and bad. In this moving scene, one senses that these eleven men, minus Judas, were bound together by a call and a choice; he had chosen them and they had chosen him. They belonged together. Such is the biblical emphasis about both this world and the next. We are neither saved nor do we serve in isolation. Likewise in eternity, we shall be in communion with each other.

An old minister tells of the shift in his understanding of heaven. As a child he used to think of heaven as a place of golden streets, gates of pearl, and full of strangers. As the years passed, he no longer thought of heaven as filled with strangers, but increasingly filled with friends and loved ones. A beautiful Old Testament phrase used in describing the death of God's saints speaks volumes: "[He] . . . died in a good old age, . . . and *was gathered to his people, and . . .* [they] buried him" (Gen. 25:8-9).

Another query about knowledge: Do the people in heaven now remember us? Like so many other questions about the Father's house, the answer involves the Scriptures and common sense. We speak often of God's love, and some things we can assume from his love. Hebrews tells us we are surrounded by a great cloud of witnesses and that they are incomplete without us. It appears that the Christian dead are in heaven, that they know it, and that they know us. They are still interested in the course of events on earth. What a great thrill awaits those Christians who die before the return of Jesus. They see the course of history from God's viewpoint! We have no reason to assume they no longer care about us, that they who surround God's throne have forgotten us for whom they prayed daily and with whom they toiled and witnessed for the Master. In Revelation 5, we find the beautiful and dramatic scene in which the golden bowls of the prayers of the saints are poured out on the altar. Surely those prayers were mingled prayers of saints both above and here below.

A most godly woman in my congregation recently passed on to be with the Father. No longer will she be praying daily in her earthly home for her pastor. No longer will I receive her long-distance phone call just before I go to the pulpit at revivals and speaking engagements, telling me of her prayerful support. But it is unthinkable that she is no longer making intercession for her pastor and others before God's throne!

Further meditation upon our heavenly home leads to the theme of *change* and *discontinuity*. Some aspects of earthly experience will continue, but others will definitely have no place in heaven. As we earlier recognized many bridges between the two worlds, so now we see some glorious differences.

There will be no sorrow there. "God shall wipe away all tears from their eyes; and there shall be no more death, neither sorrow, nor crying, neither shall there be any more pain: for the former things are passed away" (Rev. 21:4). The ultimate cause of our sorrow is sin. Not always or perhaps usually the direct result of our own sin; yet sorrow is the conclusion of the chain of sin set in motion in the Garden and reenacted in each of our lives. There will be no sin in heaven and, therefore, no sorrow.

Yet the Bible does not endorse a cheap, eternal happiness in heaven based on indifference or amnesia. The blessedness of knowing ourselves, God, and the world from God's vantage point will overwhelm our sense of sorrow. We will, indeed, "understand it better by and by."

There will be no sin in heaven. We have already seen the connection of sin and sorrow. Not only does the sinlessness of heaven mean there will be no sorrow in the celestial city but it also signals the end of our constant struggle with our sin. That is good news for those who long to rise above sinful, rebellious self! It is good news for those who look from afar on lovely ideals that escape our grasp! It is good news for those who are chained here to a dream of what should be and could be, a dream constantly dashed by sin! "O wretched man that I am! who shall deliver me from the body of this death? I thank God through Jesus Christ our Lord" (Rom. 7:24-25). In heaven we shall be sinless, unshackled, set free!

There will be no corruption in the Father's house. When I think upon this aspect, I remember Credence's fear in *The*

Pilgrim's Progress about whether there would be children in heaven. The British Two Minutes Silence for the war dead comes echoing back:

They shall not grow old, as we that are left
    shall grow old:
Age shall not weary them, nor the years condemn.
At the going down of the sun and in the morning,
We will remember them.

Time shall be no more. No longer will the years, like an ever-moving stream, bear all her children away. In that celestial city, there is no shadow of an end. This children's poem states it well:

> The stars shine over the earth,
> The stars shine over the sea;
> The stars look up to the Mighty God,
> The stars look down on me.
> The stars shall live for a million years,
> A million years and a day;
> But God and I will live and love
> When the stars have passed away.

Three pictures of the glory of heaven stand at the close of the Bible. The conflict, rebellion, sin, and sorrow of humanity does not end until Revelation 21. Then pictures of a tabernacle (vv. 1-8), a city (vv. 9-27), and a garden (22:1-5) come into focus.

The tabernacle is the symbol of God's presence with his people. The sea is gone (ch. 4); there is no more separation from God. The beautiful city has walls to symbolize security; God's people need never fear anything again. The gates in the wall are symbolized through pearls, produced through suffering. And every pilgrim who enters the Holy City understands that the gates swing open only because one who is the Pearl of great price suffered on earth for us. The garden is in stark contrast to that wrecked Garden with which the Bible begins. This last garden is made possible by him who agonized in a garden in the middle of the Bible and went to his cross for us.

We enter heaven, where God is, not by a road map but by a spiritual decision of commitment to Jesus.

5

The Hallowing of God's Name

John 17:1-6

Our Father who art in heaven, *Hallowed be thy name*. Thy kingdom come, Thy will be done, On earth as it is in heaven. Give us this day our daily bread; And forgive us our debts, As we also have forgiven our debtors; And lead us not into temptation, But deliver us from evil (Matt. 6:9-13).

Surely this first phrase is the most misunderstood phrase in the Lord's Prayer. It is not merely that children often mishear the words, as when a preschooler lisps, "Our Father . . . . how do you know my name?" Even when we know the right words, we may miss the *intent* of the phrase. I've wondered how many folk know that *good-bye* is the bestowal of a blessing and a prayer: God be with you!

Martin Luther said that no other petition in the prayer so destroys our present existence as this one. In light of that, let's examine the individual words, then seek the intent of the phrase.

Name

What's in a name? Why should God's name be special? Are we being carried back to the ancient idea that name and character are intertwined? That's certainly not true today! I know a lot of folk named Smith, but most of them have never seen a blacksmith's forge. Do any Millers you know operate a grist mill? Does Mr. Cooper make barrels? Does Christopher bear a cross? Is Margaret a pearl or Dora a true gift, or Irene always peaceful?

Does God have a name? He must because most of us would find it impossible to worship a "first cause," or "ground of being," or "mother nature." Obviously God's name is consistent with his righteous character, even if our names aren't. We are told in the Old Testament: "Those who know thy name put their trust in thee, for thou, O Lord, hast not forsaken those who seek thee" (Ps. 9:10, RSV).

There are hints of God's name in his creation. The majestic monotony of the pounding waves on the seashore and the mountains dressed in crimson and gold hint of a name with power and beauty. When we read Jesus' words about Solomon not being clothed in splendor matching the common lily or when we watch a skein of geese wheeling overhead, we know God's name has something to do with caring and order.

But isn't nature red in tooth and claw? The thoughtful person sees both beauty and beast in nature. As Christians, we know this is a result of what we call the Fall. That tendency to rebel, chronicled in the opening chapters of Genesis, has permeated all of nature, bringing about conflict and bondage and decay. To see God's hand and name in nature, we must be able to recognize as well the tragic results of our sinfulness, both individually and corporately.

God's name is more clearly revealed in the Old Testament than in nature. When Abraham led his beloved child, Isaac, up the mountain in the land of Moriah and prepared to sacrifice his dearest and best, God revealed more of his name in his deliverance. "And Abraham called the name of that place Jehovah-jireh [Jehovah will provide]" (Gen. 22:14).

When Moses, comfortable with living on the backside of nowhere, was told that he had to confront Pharoah and the Hebrew slaves, his response was to ask God for his name as backup power. God's response was, "I am That I Am" (Ex. 3:14). Gideon learned a deeper expression of God's name in his victory over Baalism. On the same night in which he was to destroy the pagan altar of his father, Gideon was visited by an angel of Jehovah and strengthened with an inner peace. He built an altar and "called it Jehovah-shalom": Jehovah is peace (Judg. 6:24).

But God's name is seen, revealed, and heard best in the New Testament. "I have manifested thy name unto the men whom thou gavest me out of the world" (John 17:6). The name of God is Jesus. In Jesus we see God's character and personality as never before or since. Apart from Jesus, there is no clear name for God, no clarity of character. To be sure, God is more than could be crammed into time and space, into the sinew and bone, flesh and blood of a man. But what people saw in Jesus was purely God.

So the name of God is that One in the midst of the crowd at the synagogue in Nazareth, interpreting the Scriptures. God's name is that same One in the midst of a crowd, healing the sick and demon-possessed, saying there is no relationship, no peace with the powers of evil. God's name is that same One, eating with outcasts and sinners, saying that our Heavenly Father forgives us.

Hallowed

We must remember that the word *hallowed* is kin to the root word in the New Testament translated in its various forms as "separated," "saint," "holy," "set apart." Someone has said the first four Commandments are commentary on the word *hallowed:* You shall have no other gods; no images; no empty use of the divine name; and keep the sabbath sacred. Indeed, these must be obeyed for God's name to be *hallowed* or set apart.

Have we lost our sense of God's holiness, his hallowedness? If we have lost our sense of respect and awe for his Word and his house, we are saying these don't relate to his "set-apartness." Most likely the chatter that is heard in many churches before worship services begin is a sign that the hallowedness is leaving his house.

I confess to a deep feeling of awe and sense of God's presence in our church as the service begins. Worshipers sharing by television first see the great arch and columns of the baptistry, then the scene broadens to include the majestic architecture of the pulpit area. This is God's house, and I find Isaiah's experience in God's house coming unbidden to my mind.

Every place of worship is God's house.

Every time we enter (or even pass by) we ought to be filled with a sense of reverence, quietness, prayer. Somewhere I read of a crippled saint whose ministry was that of constant prayer for her church's leaders. She ended each prayer with, "And may he be silent before thee!"

What is true of the place of worship dedicated to God is surely as true of other aspects of his plan for the ages. There ought to be a set-apartness about prayer, about witnessing, about worship, about Bible study, and about the daily life of we who belong to God.

Intent

This prayer is not asking the Lord to make his name holy; it already is. Neither is the prayer suggesting that *we* can make God's name holy. That is beyond our power. Let us paraphrase part of the prayer: Our Father, who art in heaven, let your name, your character, your love be recognized and have influence in the affairs of men, and I place my life before you to be a tool for that purpose.

Does not this prayer, and especially this petition, fit far better on the lips of the prodigal son than on the lips of the smooth Pharisees? Here we seem to catch a whisper of one whose life and desires have not always been in keeping with the set-apartness of God's will for people. Stumbling into the light from the darkness, beating upon their breasts as the publican, sensing the radical cleavage between the best of our human righteousness and God's holiness, sinners may offer their lives to God in this petition. It is a prayer fit for fresh offering each day to God from every child of his.

Certain implications arise from placing our lives before God to be used in this world to make known his character. First, we are saying this is a pagan world, else no need to pray such a prayer. Our vision of God, as his children, rises above a pagan world like a mountain above a plain. Secondly, God must do the hallowing of his name, for profane people cannot.

How will God hallow his name? How does God hallow his name daily in your life and mine and in this world through us? *God is hallowed in my life to the extent I allow the Holy Spirit to shape my understanding of God's character, and his will for all people through Christ.* God is only hallowed in my life when my beliefs about him are consistent with his revealed character. I must not represent God in the mold of the old Greek gods who partook of all the sins of the world, merely with greater appetite. If I am a bigoted, overfed, complacent Christian, I represent God as being the keeper of a bigoted, prejudiced people. If I am more concerned about proper food for my pet than about the starving millions, then I am saying God's nature is that of a god of the overfed, uncaring Americans. If I am not careful, I picture my God as one who dotes on America and laughs at the rest of a dying world.

People recognize God's character, love, and influence in the affairs of people when Christians clearly reflect his character. When our words and actions imply that God loves some people more than others or that God winks at sin or that God is weaker than money, then I am not being used to hallow God's name. I am profaning his name! I am scribbling obscenities on the walls of his creation.

Can it be that we who call ourselves by Christ's name are open to the charge John Wesley leveled at some religious folk, "Your God is my devil!" Paul gave the church much to reflect upon when, in Romans 2, he rebuked the Jews, saying the name of God was blasphemed among the Gentiles because of them!

God does not want us to rush out and do anything but first simply be still, be still and recognize our sinfulness and his grace freely offered. We need to recognize our betrayal of him, and his forgiveness, then freshly commit ourselves to be used of him.

6
"Thy Kingdom Come"

Luke 13:18-29

Our Father who art in heaven, Hallowed be thy name. *Thy kingdom come,* Thy will be done, On earth as it is in heaven. Give us this day our daily bread; And forgive us our debts, As we also have forgiven our debtors; And lead us not into temptation, But deliver us from evil (Matt. 6:9-13, RSV).

It was his first message; it was his central message. It was steady like the ticking of a clock, refreshing like the soft spring breeze; but sometimes it became solemn as a funereal tolling of a bell or as jarring as the shriek of a fire alarm.

"No one who puts his hand to the plow and looks back is fit for the kingdom of God" (Luke 9:62). The twelve and the seventy were sent forth to preach, heal, and to say, "The kingdom of heaven is at hand" (Matt. 10:7). The disciples were told to seek first the kingdom of God (Matt. 6:33). The kingdom of God is likened to a mustard seed, leaven, treasure hid in a field, a pearl

69

of great price, a fisherman's net, and a householder—all in one chapter (Matt. 13)!

To the crowds Jesus said, ''There shall be weeping and gnashing of teeth, when ye shall see Abraham, and Issac, and Jacob, and all the prophets, in the kingdom of God, and yourselves thrust out. And they shall come from the east, and from the west, and from the north, and from the south, and shall sit down in the kingdom of God'' (Luke 13:28-29).

Yet the kingdom of God is never defined. Although it is mentioned forty-nine times in Matthew, sixteen times in Mark, and thirty-eight times in Luke, there is no clear definition. What did Jesus mean when he spoke of the kingdom of God? We cannot pray, ''Thy kingdom come'' until we know the answer to that question. He didn't mean what contemporary rabbis meant and what the religious Jew had in mind. They were waiting for the Messiah to come, breaking into history and blowing the horn of freedom which would gather all the Jews to Palestine. The Messiah would usher in a time of material glory, unparalleled culinary pleasures, and a lifetime of a thousand years for his people. And in this golden age, the Gentiles would serve tables. This picture was not Jesus' idea of the kingdom of God.

He didn't mean God's rule over a patch

of land. We may speak of the British Empire, upon which in the nineteenth century the sun never set, as being the kingdom of Queen Elizabeth. But the statements of Jesus about the kingdom of God are different from such ideas.

Jesus seemed to speak of the kingdom of God as God's rule over people's lives, God's rule in their hearts, rather than a reign over an area. To enter the kingdom of God is to seek to do his will as a child of his. Before Jesus, no one ever fully desired or did God's will; since Jesus, no one has ever fully desired or done God's will. In Jesus of Nazareth, the kingdom of God was manifest in its completeness, its purity, and its power.

When we see this connection between the kingdom of God and God's rule in our individual hearts, the sayings, parables, and pictures of the New Testament are much more clearly focused. As a person, I am confronted with the kingdom when I am challenged to accept or reject God's will in my life. So the kingdom is not a country I can locate on a map and visit; rather it is dynamic and confronts me with God's gifts and demands. The kingdom of God does begin with an invitation (Luke 14) from God to accept his will as we perceive it in Jesus.

The kingdom of God demands repentance; a change of direction. That is why we must pray, "*Thy* kingdom come" That is why Paul, when struck down on the Damascus road, asked what Jesus wanted him to do.

The kingdom of God is a small entity; it begins afresh in every heart and grows and grows. Jesus said it was like the mustard seed. So one can, indeed, be "not far from the kingdom of God." We can tremble on the brink of commitment, fearful as we see both the past and the future, yet aware of the paralyzing power of indecision. How was it put by the Master: no man, putting his hand to the plow and then looking back; no man can serve two masters? An unknown poet phrased it thus:

> Heaven's gates are open wide;
> still the gypsies camp outside.

I cannot enter the kingdom of God unless I make a radical, about-face decision to make his way mine—without reservations, without a rival.

The kingdom is clearly a mixed situation from our human viewpoint, made so by the challenge and the invitation. Some will follow a little way, for a little time. We read the parables of the wheat and the tares, the good and trash fish, and realize not everyone who says, "Lord, Lord," is willing to follow.

We may go further still. Jesus' theme is,

"Thy kingdom come, Thy will be done"—at any cost or effort. For the kingdom is worth all our striving. That much-debated saying in Luke 16:16 is lighted up by the glow of the kingdom as God's rule in our hearts: "The law and the prophets were until John; since then the good news of the kingdom of God is preached, and every one enters it violently." The kingdom of God is only for those who see the tyranny of self-rule, who are desperate men and women, who force their way. As James Denny once said, "The kingdom of God is not for the well-meaning but for the desperate." Jesus said he came not to save the self-righteous, but those who were spiritually sick. Gethsemane shows us that the will of God is not easy to seek or to claim when it is found. Without tears, the decision to enter the kingdom is scarcely made; without tears, it is scarcely understood. Thy kingdom come—not partly, not later—in my life.

We haven't always shot straight with you from the pulpit, you know. We have said that salvation, God's presence, God's rule in your life was free. Like all half-truths, that is exceedingly dangerous. To enter the kingdom, to gain the pearl of great price, can and may cost me my material possessions, my dreams and ambitions, friends and acquaintances.

The kingdom of God is a kingdom of

two moments. In Jesus, the kingdom of God came in its fullness, but it was a pattern we saw. The universal fullness, the consummation of God's rule over all his creation is yet to come. The individual rule of God in the hearts of each of his subjects will someday be universal, sweeping over all his creation.

But not yet. For two thousand years those who love God have prayed, "Thy kingdom come." Generations of saints have come and gone, and the mustard seed has not yet become the great tree, but it shall come to pass. "At the name of Jesus every knee should bow, of things in heaven, and things in earth, and things under the earth; And that every tongue should confess that Jesus Christ is Lord, to the glory of God the Father" (Phil. 2:10-11).

Even though the full bloom of the kingdom may wait for a thousand years more, it is closer today than yesterday. On the beaches of time, our Lord's footsteps are drawing near to where we build our sand castles and throw mud.

Jesus shall reign where'er the sun
Does his successive journeys run;
His kingdom spread from shore to shore,
Till moons shall wax and wane no more.

From north to south the princes meet
To pay their homage at his feet;

While western empires own their Lord,
And savage tribes attend his word.

To him shall endless pray'r be made,
And endless praises crown his head;
His name like sweet perfume shall rise
With ev'ry morning sacrifice.

People and realms of ev'ry tongue
Dwell on his love with sweetest song,
And infant voices shall proclaim
Their early blessings on his name.

Isaac Watts

But not yet, for the kingdom is a quiet, growing wonder. Our task is to behold the kingdom growing in our own lives. A couple of summers ago I vacationed in Scotland. I saw in David Livingstone's birthplace at High Blantyre the diary in which he made these words as a last entry: "My Jesus, my king, my life, my all—I again dedicate myself to Thee." It is told that Jonathan Edwards declared, "I go out to preach with two propositions in mind: one, every person here ought to give his life to Christ; two, whether or not anyone else gives him their life—I will give him mine."

7
"Thy Will Be Done"

Mark 3:31-35

Our Father who art in heaven, Hallowed be thy name. Thy kingdom come, *Thy will be done, On earth as it is in heaven.* Give us this day our daily bread; And forgive us our debts, As we also have forgiven our debtors; And lead us not into temptation, But deliver us from evil (Matt. 6:9-13, RSV).

It was an Easter morning nearly twenty years ago. We had concluded the sunrise service in the little cemetery behind the village church and had come into the church basement for coffee and doughnuts. I looked out one of the windows and saw, standing out in the cemetery, a dear friend weeping over the grave of his six-year-old son whose funeral I had held the first week I had come to pastor the church. I went outside to seek to comfort him. "It's God's will," he said.

A couple of weeks after, a train was speeding down the tracks at the little crossing no more than 100 yards from the church on a Sunday morning. A woman driving the car, with windows rolled up, and several children talking, didn't see the train or hear its whistle. In the heartbreaking aftermath of that tragedy one heard the comment on all sides, "It was God's will."

But, is it God's will? Is that the time and is that the place when we ought to say, quote, or pray, "Thy will be done"? When we lay these kind of things at the throne of God, I feel deeply burdened. I believe that when we lay these terrible events at the throne of God, what we are really saying is that we do not think we can bear the weight of this terrible event unless somehow we can say, "This is God's will."

But if that's really the way it is, does that not mean that the will of God is nothing more than blind fate or chance? Do we not then have to agree with Robert Browning's "Paracelsus" as he speaks his mind to the friend who has just given him that kind of line:

Now, 't is I most admire—/The constant talk men of your stamp keep up/Of God's will, as they style it; one would swear/Man had but merely to uplift his eye,/And see the will in question charactered/On heaven's vault. . . ./ . . ./I know as much of any will of God/As knows some dumb and tortured brute what Man,/His stern lord, wills from the perplexing

blows/That plague him every way; but there, of
course,/Where least he least suffers, longest he
remains—/My case; and for such reasons I plod
on,/subdued, but not convinced.[1]

Is God's will to simply be joined with
fate, chance, and all the terrible things that
happen to us? There are basically two questions involved in the matter.

The first question is, *What do we perceive to be the will of God.* The second question is, *How do we relate our lives to that
which we perceive to be the will of God.*

How do we perceive, how do we define
God's will? We must let our perspective be a
Godward perspective and not a human-
centered perspective. Too often we approach this matter of what is God's will by
asking, What is *my* will? But we must seek
God's will for this universe, God's will for
your life and mine.

Our reversal of this approach has given
us curious terminology! For instance, when
the snowflakes softly fall, when the warm
spring rains come, when the flowers un-
fold, when the summer breezes blow, and
the grain fields ripple, we speak of the glory
of "mother nature." That is because what is
happening fits in with what *we want* to happen. But when the tornado comes, when

the hurricane sweeps, when the earthquake rumbles, then we say, "It is an act of *God*." We say it is God's will because it is *contrary* to our will.

Let's start from God's perspective. What is God's will? God's will is that all come to accept Christ as Lord and Savior. In Romans 8:28, we find God's will stated in more theological terms. We read that God is working all things together for good to those who love him, to them who are called according to his purpose. And we find that it is those who love him who are the called ones. For those whom he foreknew, he also predestined to be conformed to the image of his Son. We read in the earlier part of the eighth chapter that, through this creation of a new race of people like Jesus, God's intention is to reclaim his creation by working his Spirit through sons and daughters like Jesus. God's intention, his will, is to reclaim every erring child and to recreate his twisted creation; to restore, to set back straight his creation from the blight of sin which it has experienced.

The Bible tells us that this magnificent will of God shall be done in the end. It may not be done *in* my small life, for I can close my life to God. If I close my life to the working of God, his will may not be done *through* my life, as a blessing to others. But it *shall be done.* This is the confident thrust of the Bible.

How does that fit in, then, with the individual events in my life? Is everything that happens God's will? Are all the sicknesses God's will? Are all the accidents God's will? Are all the tragedies God's will?

Keep in mind that we are talking about God's will for creation. Remember two things. First, remember that *God never wills evil.* God is love, truth, caring, life, beauty. God is not evil. God does no evil. The character of God must be defined not by our imagination but by Jesus. God is like Jesus.

Remember also that the *tragic results of our sin are constantly with us.* Much of the sickness and sorrow, much of the misfortune and tragedy of this world, can be traced back to the twisted net in which we find ourselves because of our own sin, because of the sin of others, and because of the corporate sin of this world. We have twisted God's creation. Therefore, much of what happens to us is due to the sin around us. It is a terrible thing to say of an act that is a result of sin, "This is the will of God."

So, when we speak of God's will, let us have a clear image of God's intention for this world. Let us not use individual, terrible events in our lives as a starting point. We

will see God's intention most rightly understood when we see it working out in the life
of Jesus. "I am come that they might have
life, and that they might have it more abun-
dantly" (John 10:10). If we look at the broad
outlines of Jesus' life, we find that *he was
against evil* at every turn. We find that *he
was for people* everywhere. We also find
that *he was totally committed to God.* That
is the picture of God's will.

So, the answer to the question, What do
we perceive to be God's will? is what we see
in Jesus. God wills that this creation be re-
structured and brought back to him; God
wills that every erring child be rescued. And,
once rescued, he wills to work through us
as part of a new people like Jesus.

If that is God's will, how do I relate my
life to it? Again, we must answer the question by looking at it from God's intention.
We begin by saying it is impossible to know
or to have God's will done in our lives unless we are regenerated, born again, unless
we are Christians. There is no way lost people can have God's will done in their lives.

God's will in our lives begins with a saving acceptance of the One in whom the kingdom of God was fleshed out: Jesus Christ.
Only by our surrender of our lives to him can
we know God's will. *Then we shall see
whether a particular event is a terrible shat-*

tering of our dreams or a result of our commitment to God.

If we follow the model of Jesus, we find that God's will is done in our lives when every area is turned over to him and when all the faculties of our lives are used in seeking that which is his will. Jesus, for instance, found God's will by the use of his *mind*. Jesus saw the sorrow and pain of disease and battled it without respite. We often contradict ourselves in times of illness. We beg trained doctors to do something about a terrible illness and would give a fortune for a cure. Then, when the disease runs it horrible course, we say wearily, "It was God's will." Jesus used his logical mind to fight disease and evil. He used his *conscience*, as when he turned over the tables of the money changers in the Temple. He used his *friends* to determine God's will, as when he asked of the twelve in seclusion, "Whom do men say that I . . . am?" (Matt. 16:13). He turned to *prayer* to find God's will in his life, spending whole nights alone with God. He turned to the *Scriptures* to find God's will, as in the temptations when he quoted Scripture verses back to Satan.

If we seek to have God's will done in our lives, what can we expect? Again look at the life of Jesus. We may expect lives of large purpose and scope. That does not mean that our lives will be highly acclaimed but they will be lives which will bring glory to God and which will be used in achieving his purpose for this world. This will be a costly way to live. There will be no special treatment or protection.

An unknown poet put it this way: "Does the road wind uphill all the way? Yes, to the very end. Will the day's journey take the whole day? From morning till night."

To pray, "Thy will be done" means, however, that God's children can steadfastly pray in the midst of troubles, knowing that God's will is good. We know we will have his fellowship and that somewhere there is light, though it may be dark in our valleys. We can know, too, that someday Satan will be defeated and all the crooked things will be made straight.

Consider the last phrase, "Thy kingdom come, Thy will be done, *On earth as it is in heaven*." How often we have sought to make of religion an otherworldly thing, an otherworldly phenomenon, pie in the sky, by-and-by. But this prayer brings religion down to earth: "On earth as it is in heaven." On the whole earth, from shore to shore, around the globe. That also means in the places where we live. Thy will be done on earth through me, through my commitment to thee.

The Bible has a beautiful scene of what God's will is like in heaven. That scene will one day be reflected upon the earth. In Revelation 4 and 7, we have the vision of heaven given to John. What do we see in these pictures? We see the magnificent throne of God, the blood-washed host, and the Lamb of God. We see the bright band of messengers waiting to do God's bidding. We see heaven ringing with praises to God. The scenes of heaven which the Bible gives us are scenes of trust, obedience, fellowship, and peace. That is what God wants on earth, as he works out his will through you and me.

Archibald Rutledge has a story about an old, black turpentine worker and his dog. The turpentine worker always brought his lunch pail to work. He would set the pail down by a tree and bid his old dog guard it carefully until lunchtime. One day, while the crew was working a good distance from the lunches, a forest fire broke out between the men and the lunches. When they were finally able to make their way back to the camp, the entire area was a smoking, ravaged scene. The old black man went over and knelt down by the remains of his old dog. As tears coursed down his leathery cheeks, he was heard to say, "I always had to be careful what I tol' him to do 'cause I knowed he'd do it." Can God say that about you and me? That's what his will is all about.

Note

1. Browning, Robert. *Poetical Works of Browning*, "Paracelsus" Cambridge Edition, Houghton Mifflin Co., Boston, 1895 (play).

8
"Our Daily Bread"

John 6:33-35

Our Father who art in heaven, Hallowed be thy name. Thy kingdom come, Thy will be done, On earth as it is in heaven. *Give us this day our daily bread;* And forgive us our debts, As we also have forgiven our debtors; And lead us not into temptation, But deliver us from evil (Matt. 6:9-13, RSV).

The crying need of our times is *not* for the church of the living God to give this weary world more facts about Jesus of Nazareth. Our unbelieving neighbor already knows more gospel than he believes! What is needed is not more facts, but persuasion. The unbelieving neighbor wants to see the power and the presence of the Lord Jesus demonstrated in your life and mine. He wants to know if there's anything to the facts he has heard since childhood. He wants to see the power and the presence of Jesus *demonstrated.* He wants to see immoral people become moral; unethical people become ethical. He wants to see people forgiven of sin and cleansed from iniquity. *If* it works, then he'd like to have it. If you have found bread from heaven, then he'd like to have it too. But as long as we say we have bread and yet starve spiritually, he questions what we say.

Jesus' disciples found themselves in the same kind of crisis that the church finds itself in many times today: a world asking for proof, waiting for demonstration of the truth. We all remember the story of Jesus and his chosen disciples Peter, James, and John on the mount of transfiguration. The account ends with their descent to the foot of the mountain to find a young boy foaming at the mouth in the throes of some seizure. The other disciples stood helpless, unable to heal the boy. Later, off to the side, they said to Jesus, "Why could not we cast him out? And he said unto them, This kind can come forth by nothing, but by prayer" (Mark 9:28-29). The secret of Jesus' power and presence was prayer. If we, his modern disciples, would have power, we must be people of prayer. To empower the twelve, Jesus gave the Model Prayer. If we can make this prayer ours, we can be used of God.

We now come to the fifth part of the Model Prayer. We have found the first four phrases to be packed with power. Every

phrase is, as it were, a creed; every phrase is
doctrine, faith, and life.

To understand the significance of this
present portion, we must use the first four
phrases as backdrop. A paraphrase might
read something like this:

Our Father, who art in heaven: *the one who
prays this with understanding realizes through
Jesus Christ who the Father is, and who we are.*
Hallowed be thy name: *the one who prays this
with understanding is saying, "Father, may thy
character, thy love, thy will be seen and have
influence in the affairs of men and thereto I
place my life before thee."* Thy Kingdom come:
*when we thus pray, understanding that his
Kingdom is not a rule over a land mass, but his
rule in the hearts of his children, then we lay ourselves before his throne saying, "I am thine, O
Lord!"* Thy Will be done: *when we pray this
with understanding, we are saying, "I shall be
partner in bringing to fruition the great intention
of God for this twisted world and for his run-
away children."*

These are high and holy concepts.
When we make them ours, we feel that we
are in a cathedral with beautiful stained-
glass windows, high, vaulted ceilings, full
of beauty and glory.

Then it seems as if, in the midst of the
singing of the doxology in this cathedral, a
beggar comes down the main aisle. It

seems as if, among all these high, soaring-eagle phrases of holiness, we are suddenly interrupted by a sparrow or worse yet, by a pigeon that pecks his beak along on the sidewalk looking for a crust of bread.

For in the midst of all these holy concepts, "Our Father who art in heaven, Hallowed be thy name, Thy kingdom come, Thy will be done, On earth as it is in heaven," we are brought back to the everyday. *"Give us now our daily bread,"* is like a pigeon in the midst of eagles.

But handle those words gently. Those words are filled with explosive power. He who honestly prays, "Give us this day our daily bread," may not understand what he is saying.

There are at least four explosive questions beneath the surface of what has been popularly called the "cupboard petition." First is the question concerning our daily bread: *Does God really care about my everyday needs*? The second question is about the idea of daily bread: *How much is enough daily*? Then, *for whom am I responsible*? And *are we really dependent upon God*?

Let's take these questions one at a time. First, Does God care about my daily needs? Yes. God does, indeed, care. I think we must sail through a narrow strait in this matter.

There are churches and religious groups who would take advantage of our hunger for material things and our weakness for superstition. They would guarantee that if people have a certain kind or quality of faith they can have all the material goods their hearts desire. These churches and religious groups, among whom are honest believers as well as charlatans, would offer a sop of a magic handkerchief to our souls. We must sail between that kind of materialism on the one hand and those churches which would be ultraspiritual and would not even mention such things as the church financial budget on the other hand.

There is a middle ground. Nothing is secular; all this world is sacred before God. I fear we have too often divided life into secular and sacred, spiritual and material, and tried to save people's souls while letting their bodies go to hell. The Salvation Army quickly learned that this must not be done. For if the freezing person's knees are knocking badly, if the starving person's stomach is growling so loudly, then they cannot hear the preaching of the good news of Jesus!

God does care about our daily needs. Jesus' first temptation had to do with daily need; the tempter's first thrust had to do not with the high and lofty will of God for humanity, but with the mundane, practical, and pressing need for bread to stem Jesus' own hunger. And even as he felt hunger, no doubt gaunt legions rose up before him, the starving people of his land. On every street, the ever-present starving beggars, pleading for a crust—for God's sake. In the wilderness, Jesus determined not to misuse the power given him. Yet he was concerned for people's physical needs. Yes, God cares about our everyday, common needs.

But I think we must put these everyday, common needs in the same framework with the more "spiritual" needs. That means simply this, that as we pray for everyday, common needs we must ask, Is this a worthy prayer? If it is, pray it! We must ask, Have we done all we can, in partnership with God, to bring to pass this which is good and needful? If we have, pray it! And then must we say, God's will shall be my will, and I shall trust him in this matter, as well as in the "spiritual" matters.

The second question: How much bread is enough? You and I know that the term *bread* is used, not simply to refer to the loaf, but to all the physical needs of our lives. It is bread, the necessities of life, for which we plead, not cake. I fear we have become confused.

What are the necessities of our lives? You are well aware, as I am, that most of the

things which were called luxuries a generation ago are seen by this present generation
to be necessities! I became quite ashamed,
traveling in Southeast Asia sometime ago,
when I realized the contrast between the
way the Third World lives and the way
Americans live. All the world does not live
in the lap of luxury!

How much bread is enough? Jesus realized that people need only enough bread
to sustain them while they do God's will.
That's what those first four phrases of the
prayer teach us. We need enough bread to
enable us to do his will, to seek his kingdom, to be partners with him in bringing his
intentions to pass.

But does that mean that God does not
want my family to have nice things? Does
God want you to have an automobile when
you need it? Does God want our children to
be well educated? Does God want you to
have enough money to take a vacation?
Yes, I think God does. But there are sins that
attach themselves to bread which we must
face. Notice our question: How much is
enough? There is the sin of anxiety. Oddly
enough, either too little or too much bread
will create anxiety. Misuse of our bread
breeds anxiety.

One of Moses' farewell speeches tells
us why we're given bread. Moses reminded

the children of Israel, who were fed with manna from above in the wilderness, why God fed them:

And he humbled you and let you hunger and fed you with manna, which you did not know, nor did your fathers know; that he might make you know that man does not live by bread alone, but that man lives by everything that proceeds out of the mouth of the Lord. Your clothing did not wear out upon you, and your foot did not swell, these forty years (Deut. 8:3-4, RSV).

God gives us bread so that we might trust in him. How tragic it is when, instead of trusting, we become anxious. When Jesus decided that he would not use his powers to gain bread for himself or anyone else, he settled for himself the matter of trust in God. It is against that backdrop we ought to read Matthew 6, in which he said, having renounced his own power to live independently of God, "Seek ye first the kingdom of God, . . . and all these things shall be added" (v. 33). "Your Father knoweth what things ye have need of" (v. 8b).

Be not anxious, but use common sense. We need enough bread for lean times. The Israelites in the desert gathered manna on the sixth day for the seventh, and so we need to gather in the six decades for the seventh and following decades. Surely God does not frown on our saving some bread for the rainy day. I can yet remember my father, an insurance salesman, being chagrined over a conversation he had with a minister when I was just a child. I remember him coming home and telling my mother that the preacher was not using common sense, assuming that to buy insurance is wrong and a sign of lack of faith in God.

But there is another sin that attaches itself to bread: the sin of selfishness. It does not take a lot of bread to make a person selfish. Each of us must ask ourselves the basic question: Why am I living? Remember the old adage, Do you live to eat or eat to live? Do you live to make bread or do you make bread in order to live so that you may do God's will? Every Christian has to ask himself, What is the reason for my being? Is the purpose of my life to heap up bread? Or is the purpose of my life to do the will of God? Is the bread that I make to be used entirely for my needs and my family's needs, or is it also to be used to glorify God and help the needy?

The third question is: For whom am I responsible? What is meant by these plural pronouns in the Model Prayer? This *us* and *our* bread? Let me stress that when God gives bread to one, he gives bread to all. God intends that we share. That is surely the thrust of the story of Lazarus and Dives. Lazarus was a beggar who was brought daily to the gate of the rich man, Dives, who fared sumptuously. All Lazarus wanted was to eat the pieces of bread which the rich guests of Dives had cast aside after using them as napkins to wipe the gravy from their lips. That's all Lazarus wanted. While he sought to get that, the dogs came and licked his sores. What a pitiful scene. You remember that at the end of the story Lazarus went to heaven and the rich man went to hell. But it is pure speculation to say the rich man was obviously an evil man. No, the truth of the matter is the rich man's sin was simply this, he was content and complacent while his fellowman lived in poverty, need, and hopelessness!

God makes enough bread for everybody to eat; the problem is that so often you and I do not share the bread. Someone told a story about a little girl who desperately wanted a certain thing for her birthday. She prayed earnestly to God for it. But her birthday arrived and the hoped-for gift did not come. One of her little friends, chiding her, said, "See, God forgot about your gift, didn't he?"

She replied, "No, I think God told somebody else to get me that gift and they forgot about it."

God, in desiring that all his children be
fed, gives some of the bread to others to
share—and we've forgotten to share! Now
you and I cannot change whole govern-
ments. You and I cannot single-handedly
feed the teeming millions in the world who
are starving. But we can stir our own consciences. We can stir the consciences of our
churches. We can seek to have some input
in our own local situation in government.

The last question is: Are we really dependent upon God? We are to pray "give
us" because we are, indeed, dependent
upon God. Back of the loaf is the snowy
flour, back of the flour the mill, back of the
mill is the shower, the sun, and the Father's
will.

The selfish may eat in solitude and
sumptuousness, but if they think they are
not debtors, they are fools. God wants us to
understand that all we have comes from
him. We are partners. He does not mean for
us to fold our hands but to be partners with
him in providing our own food and in giving
bread to others.

When we speak only of physical bread,
we have said but the half. Jesus said, "I am
the bread of life." He gives us more than
physical food; he gives us spiritual food.
" 'For the bread of God is that which comes
down from heaven, and gives life to the

world.' They said to him, 'Lord, give us this bread always.' Jesus said to them, 'I am the bread of life; he who comes to me shall not hunger' " (John 6:33-35, RSV).

9
The Risk of Prayer

Matthew 6:14-15

Our Father who art in heaven, Hallowed be thy name. Thy kingdom come, Thy will be done, On earth as it is in heaven. Give us this day our daily bread; *And forgive us our debts, As we also have forgiven our debtors;* And lead us not into temptation, But deliver us from evil (Matt. 6:9-13, RSV).

In the midst of a busy city, directly across from a beautiful and soothing park, rise the columns and spire of a magnificent church. It is noontime and a secretary from an office complex nearby sits on a park bench. Between sips of a soft drink and bites from her sandwich lunch, she idly ponders the church. She grew up in an outlying, county-seat town. When she left home to work in the city, she left many aspects of her life at home.

She hasn't been to church lately; her friends would never know she was a professed Christian. As she munches her way through the lunch hour, the chimes in the church spire ring out the old hymns. Unexpectedly, as a thief on silent feet, a vague and uneasy feeling invades the mind of the secretary. It is a unique mix of need, loss, shame, guilt, and sin. She has come, through absent-mindedly pondering her life, to the focus of that portion of the Lord's Prayer to which we have come in our journey of prayer.

Four phrases of soaring commitment and beauty, then one of commonplace need to which a plea for forgiveness is tied. People do not live by bread alone, but by bread in closest connection with forgiveness!

Forgive us our debts, as we forgive our debtors. A torrent of questions rush into our minds as we face this phrase: How can I honestly pray, or lay any claim to God, when I am so entangled in unforgiveness? Is it possible to desperately want to be God's child, to want to do his will, and yet also to want revenge, to be filled with anger and maybe even hatred? Will God forgive me even if I *don't* forgive others? How can I really find the power and the desire to forgive those who have hurt me deeply?

These questions all focus, like the rays of the sun burning down through a magnifying glass, upon this phrase of the prayer: *"Forgive us as we forgive those who tres-*

pass against us" (author's). This is the only phrase in the prayer upon which Jesus elaborated (see Matt. 6:9-15).

Is forgiveness necessary? Does everybody need forgiving? John Donne spoke of the fabric of the community:

No man is an island entire of itself; every man is a piece of the continent, a part of the main. If a clod be washed away by the sea, Europe is the less. . . . any man's death diminishes me, because I am involved in mankind; and therefore never send to know for whom the bell tolls; it tolls for thee!

The same community interrelatedness is true in terms of the web of sin. There is none righteous; no, not a single one! The Bible shows its greatest men standing in need of forgiveness. We have merely to recall the disobedience of Moses, David's sin with Bathsheba, Jonah's pride and prejudice, or Peter's denial of Christ. First John tells us that "If we say that we have no sin, we deceive ourselves, and the truth is not in us" (1 John 1:8). This prayer doesn't let us plead for forgiveness *if* we need it; all of us sin. Everybody needs to be forgiven; everybody knows somebody who needs forgiveness. Indeed, bread alone is not sufficient; the cattle in the barn have bread enough and to spare, yet the stall needs periodic cleaning.

Every Christian whose relationship to Christ goes deeper than his initial conversion must ponder the effects of sin within his own heart. With bitter cry we have to ask, Is the proportion of hate and unforgiveness out in the world any greater than the proportion within my heart? What child of God does not anguish over the realization that God's great plan and intention for this world is slowed down and shunted aside by evil and hatred of all kinds—and our sin adds to that dark strength! "Against thee, thee only, have I sinned, and done this evil in thy sight" (Ps. 51:4). Our lukewarmness, hypocrisy, greed, cowardice, and prejudice may be directed toward others, but in reality we drive the shaft into the heart of God.

But there is hope, love, and power in forgiveness. "Forgive us . . . as we forgive . . ." Forgiveness is neither easy nor cheap. In my opinion, the old idea of forgiving and forgetting is urged upon us only by deceivers or those who have never taken their own advice!

The sting can be pulled, but the blotting out of what may be one of your life's most traumatic experiences is an entirely different matter. Yet the act of forgiveness has tremendous power to set us free. If I may be

personal, this truth was for years an aca-
demic matter. Then came a time when I was
bitterly hurt by persons I trusted. After carry-
ing the fiendish monkey of unforgiveness
on my back for over a year, I was finally
able to accept enough grace from our Lord
to be mature enough to forgive. I have seldom felt such freedom! Nothing can• ever
blot out the knowledge and memory of that
experience except death; yet the goodwill
and ability to love in Christ were restored.

Forgiveness means being delivered
from guilt and the power of our sinful acts. It
means the restoration of relationships; it
means being filled with the desire to re-
spond to former enemies in love and concern. G. A. Studdert-Kennedy focuses
bluntly upon the place and power of the
church in forgiveness:

God can and does forgive us our trespasses;
but only as we forgive them that trespass
against us—that is, only as we become members of a Church really militant here on earth—
which is pledged and resolved to bear in its
own body the sin of the whole world.[1]

Studdert-Kennedy is saying that we can
experience the full power of God's forgiveness only in and through the fellowship of
the church. Only in this kind of redeemed

yet human fellowship can we share our guilt and our gratitude, find healing, and have the power to bless.

If this is a correct assessment, and I think it is, how tragic is that church which focuses only on our individual relationship to Christ, crackling with shortsighted self-ishness, divorced from the vast web of heartbreak and evil in the world. How crip-pled is its power to bless!

What is the requirement for forgiveness? It seems terribly clear and blunt: "Forgive us as we forgive those who trespass against us." We become our own judges, juries, and executioners! We have to be staggered by the boldness of asking God to imitate us: Lord, do to me as I do to others. It boils down to realizing that an *unforgiving* per-son must remain *unforgiven*. God does take us seriously, according to this prayer!

We must not think of God as holding grudges, like we do. This is an inexorable law: The only grounds on which we are able to receive God's pardon is the way we forgive others. The unforgiving heart is like a flower with a bucket over it, like a clenched fist in the presence of a plate of cookies.

Too many of us, even God's children, live like the boy in the legend of the runner.

He wanted so badly to be a great runner. He trained and trained; he ate the right foods, exercised correctly, and even carried in practice a rock tied to his waist. Then came the day of the big race. The signal was given, the runners leaped down the cinder track, and the coach strained to see his prize pupil. Unbelieving, he stared at the boy and yelled—to no avail. The lad insisted on racing with the rock tied to his waist. There was no way for him to win.

You and I must develop an attitude of daily forgiveness. We must be less sensitive to slights. Let us remember Jesus' words from the cross: "Father, forgive them; for they know not what they do" (Luke 23:34). We can enlist the power of prayer. We are told to "pray for them which despitefully use you" (Matt. 5:44).

We can be more understanding and slower to condemn and criticize. Most of us, after all, are fighting a tough battle. Let us remember that revenge, hatred, and unforgiveness are spiritual cancers. Who can forget Andy telling Amos about how he will stop the Kingfish from slapping him on the chest: "Amos, I'm going to put a stick of dynamite under my shirt, and when he slaps me—boom!—I'll blow his hand off."

Forgiveness is the most precious commodity in the world today. God's forgiveness is yours for the asking—in the right spirit.

Note

1. G. A. Studdert-Kennedy. *The Wicket Gate* (London: Hodder and Stoughton, 1923), p. 149.

10
"Lead Us Not into Temptation"

Luke 22:28-31,39-46

Our Father who art in heaven, Hallowed be thy name. Thy kingdom come, Thy will be done, On earth as it is in heaven. Give us this day our daily bread; And forgive us our debts, As we also have forgiven our debtors; *And lead us not into temptation, But deliver us from evil* (Matt. 6:9-13, RSV).

The Lord's Prayer begins at God's throne, as we kneel to pray that his name be hallowed, his kingdom come, his will be done. Then this great prayer tumbles down to where we live, down in the valleys. We find ourselves pleading for daily bread and for forgiveness of our trespasses. Then this prayer sweeps back up to glory again as it closes, "Thine is the kingdom, and the power, and the glory, for ever, Amen" (Matt. 6:13).

There is a kaleidoscope of images. As *children*, we kneel around our Father's chair and seek to do his will, to hallow his name, and see his kingdom come. But swiftly the

image changes. We are no longer children
kneeling around the chair of our Father but
travelers, or, perhaps worse yet, *vaga-
bonds*, begging for a crust of bread. Again
the scene changes, and we become *sol-
diers* who stand before the Commander
and plead not to be led into the very thick of
the battle. Then once again we come as
God's *children*, praising his name as the
prayer closes.

The Lord's Prayer speaks to three seg-
ments of time. *Today* we pray for our daily
bread. We ask him in some way, some
fashion, to untangle the snarled skein of
events of *yesterday*, praying "forgive us our
trespasses as we forgive those who trespass against us" (v. 12, author's). Then
tomorrow comes into view as we pray,
"Lead us not into temptation, lead us not
into the crucible of testing" (v. 13, author's).

In spite of the Lord's Prayer, most folk
are not concerned about temptation. Most
of us have relegated the whole business of
temptation to the realm of the ridiculous or
the humorous. We say, "I can withstand
anything but temptation!" We say, as the
great helping of pecan pie with ice cream
heaped on it is handed to us, "My, what a
temptation to my diet!" We have banished
the devil to Halloween.

Yet Jesus took the matter of the devil

and his temptations very seriously. Jesus
was tempted on every hand by the devil, by
his own disciples, by the Pharisees, and by
the lawyers. When we come to this petition,
it is almost as if these words come from the
heart and the lips of a shaken person, who
has just now stumbled back into the circle
of light from the realm of darkness. Even
now, turning and peering back into the darkness, the person sees the devil stalking in
the shadows, seeking whom he may de-
vour. The darkness is full of writhing temptations where a person's faith comes un-
glued and all principles begin to ravel at the
edges.

When we come to look honestly at this
petition of the Lord's Prayer, a multitude of
questions come to mind. "Lead us not into
temptation": Does God lead us into *temptation?* Does God tempt us? Is that what the
Bible really teaches? Is temptation sin?
Does God, then want us to sin? Is God laying
a trap for us?

On the other hand, if we say that this
word means not *temptation,* but *trial* and
testing, does that mean God doesn't really
know how strong our faith is? Why must he
test us if he knows? But when we begin to
ask those kinds of questions, we have
come at the matter from the wrong end. Let
us grab this petition from the other end and

begin with the very nature of our daily lives.

The nature of this world and our existence as Christians within it is the nature of an arena, a battleground. We are in the midst of a battle.

The same Greek word is translated either *temptation* or *testing,* depending upon the context and the sense of it. The Letter of James makes quite clear that God does not tempt us. When the word is actually used as a temptation, the devil is behind the tempting. God does not lure his people, hoping they will fall; that is the work of the devil.

When the word is used not as temptation with an evil connotation but as testing with a good sense, God is in this, that the world has to be of such a nature that people are tested and tried. If this world were not such an ethical battleground, there would be no good or evil. If this world were not set up in such a way that a Christian is tested and tried, there would be no spiritual growth. There would be no moral values, and people would be robots.

There must be those situations which have the potential for the Christian to fail. Unless there is the potential to fail, there cannot be the potential to grow. So God leads his children into situations in which he designs that his children shall grow in grace and knowledge and that the Father may be glorified. Oddly enough, it just so happens that the crucible of Satan's temptation is also often the arena of God's testing.

Look at the idea of testing and temptation. We somehow think that temptations of the devil are big, gaudy, obnoxious, terrible things that we can spot immediately. The greatest temptations are the most subtle. Most of us, if we truly want to, can escape the snare of the devil in terms of stealing, killing, and adultery (all the "biggies"). The problem comes with what we call the "little sins," the ones of which Jesus spoke.

Martin Luther was a man who knew the devil well. On at least one occasion, Luther is reputed to have thrown the inkwell at the devil! Luther phrased it very well when he said, "The greatest temptations to a man are these: goods, fame, child and wife." These lead us to dilute our allegiance to God.

Who has not done that which was not Christian because he wanted to be what he perceived was a good father, a good husband, a good child? Our culture is so set up that if we follow our culture we will betray Christ. Our problem is not the overarching, huge temptations. Our problem is that we are inclined to say, "I can love God *and* the world." Our problem is that we're inclined to say, "I can trust in my own security, *and*, I can trust in God."

Very few people shake their fist in the face of God and walk off saying, "I can go it alone." No, rather we just slowly begin to go our way alone.

Look in the life of Jesus to see the radical nature of the subtle temptation. In Mark's Gospel, we're told that at the very start of his ministry, after Jesus was baptized, the Spirit drove him into the wilderness. There he was tempted of the devil for forty days. Jesus had to begin his ministry in the crucible of temptation.

What were the temptations? The first was to turn stone into bread. What's wrong with that, especially when you're hungry? A lot of people are starving. Fifteen thousand people starve to death every day. Why didn't Jesus use his power to turn stones into bread to feed the starving world? It was tempting. But he knew that if he did that, he ran the risk of people with full stomachs and empty souls. Man does not live by bread alone.

The second temptation, no less subtle, was one in which the devil suggested Jesus cast himself off the pinnacle of the Temple. Surely, hinted Satan, angels would catch the Son of God or he would drift lightly down like a feather. All the people would see and follow. After all, do we not hear, even in church circles, that the means are unimportant; results count? Why didn't Jesus then make a circus and sideshow out of his ministry? Because, first of all, it would have been morally wrong. Then, he knew that if he focused only on the sensational he might win people's allegiance for a short time, but when the next clown came along with a bigger circus, the crowds would follow him. Jesus refused to be that kind of Messiah.

The third temptation was just as subtle as the others. The devil planted the promise that if Jesus would worship him all the world could be his. Nobody would have to know. Jesus knew that to do so would destroy his understanding of the will of the Father. It would shatter the relationship he had with the Father. So, he turned his back upon that bauble.

These kinds of subtle temptations dogged Jesus all the way through his ministry. In the Model Prayer, we find the shadow of that kind of temptation. It is the only negative petition in the prayer.

Come with me to the Last Supper. There, I believe, is the background of this petition. There, in the flickering of the candlelight, the Master stood before his disciples. He lifted the cup, broke the bread, and said to them, as he looked into each face, "Ye are they which have continued with me in my temptations [which also have been his trials and his testings]. And I appoint unto you a kingdom, as my Father hath appointed unto me" (Luke 22:28-29). And then he turned to Peter and said to him, "Simon, behold, Satan hath desired to have you, that he may sift you as wheat: But, I have prayed for thee" (Luke 22:31-32). He never told Peter, "You won't get sifted." He never told Peter, "Satan wants you, but I've cut his arms off!"

Then Jesus went out to the Mount of Olives and knelt down with the chosen three, Peter, James, and John, and said to them, "Pray, lest ye enter into temptation" (Luke 22:46). He went off and knelt down and said in great agony, "O my Father, if it be possible, let this cup pass from me" (Matt. 26:39). Did you hear it? And then, "nevertheless not as I will, but as thou wilt (v. 39). He went back to the three and found them sleeping. He woke them, told them to stay awake and pray that they enter not into temptation, and went back and prayed again the more bitterly and earnestly, "O my Father, . . . let this cup pass."

Let that scene be etched in our minds and hearts as the background of this petition. Jesus was led into the dark abyss of the garden for our sakes. He was led into the darkness, where the relationship of the Father grew faint and dim, where people can scarce stand the darkness. Even he prayed, "Oh, my Father, let it pass away." But from the garden, he went on to the even darker realm of the cross. Hanging between heaven and earth, he prayed, "Oh, my Father, why did you leave me?" (Matt. 27:46, author).

Jesus taught his disciples, you and me, to pray that we might not enter into the kind of darkness, the kind of trial, the kind of testing, and the kind of temptation into which he entered. "Pray," said he, "that your testing be not of that nature . . . that your night be not so dark, your valley be not so deep, as the one the Lord went through to find the sheep."

Even so, as we come to this phrase, we find the prayer implicitly saying that we *will* be led into situations that try our souls. The tragedy is for a Christian not even to know when he is being led into that kind of situation! What a tragedy not to know when our Christian morals and Christian ethics are slowly seeping away from us, to be blind and deaf and dumb in the face of an opportunity to witness for God.

There is another matter pointed out in this plea. It is pointed out that though we will be tried in the crucible of temptation and testing, God will supply us with the needed strength and the way of it.

> In the hour of trial,
> Jesus, plead for me,
> Lest by base denial,
> I depart from Thee.
> When Thou see'st me waver,
> With a look recall,
> Nor for fear or favor
> Suffer me to fall.
>
> With forbidden pleasures
> Would this vain world charm;
> Or its sordid treasures
> Spread to work me harm;
> Bring to my remembrance
> Sad Gethsemane,
> Or, in darker semblance,
> Cross-crowned Calvary.
>
> James Montgomery

God has provided in the midst of all the clutching of evil, in the face of all the encircling imps of hell, in the midst of the subtlest temptation, a way of escape.

A couple of summers ago my wife and I were standing at the airport in Bangkok, Thailand, thousands of miles from those who cared for us or anybody who even knew about us. We didn't know a soul. There were just the two of us. I was to speak at a conference of our missionaries in Thailand. Somebody was supposed to meet us at the airport. But nobody came forward. And then suddenly out of the midst of the sea of faces, a crudely lettered placard was thrust up bearing on it the one word: *Davis.* Beneath the waving hand was a smiling face. Suddenly the situation was changed from one of total ignorance and apprehension to one of guidance and help. God has provided for us in all of our situations of testing and trial. When the devil gets next to you, there will be an angel to raise a placard!

The first phrase, "lead us not into temptation," is the same as praying, "O my Father, let this cup pass." But let us remember the word, "nevertheless," in the garden. "Nevertheless, thy will be done." That is the same as saying, "Nevertheless, if I must be led into testing, then deliver thou me from the evil one." Deliver us from Satan. Some people can build their lives with neither God nor Satan in it, but not the Christian. "Deliver us from the evil one."

Our deliverance may be seen as we follow Jesus in Gethsemane. It is as if we hear him saying, "My Father, let this cup pass, but if that's not possible, then simply let thy child be preserved in the midst of the wiles of the evil one. Let him not have me. Thy will be done, thy kingdom come, thy child

be preserved." God has said he shall pre-
serve us.

Our deliverance may be seen in the life
of the local business woman who resigns
a lucrative position because her Christian
ethics and the ethics of her company could
no longer walk side by side. Our deliverance
may be seen in the life of a businessman
who is a sales manager, who must travel a
lot, and who is faithful to his family and his
wife. By so doing, he experiences Christian
growth in his witness. Our deliverance may
be seen in the life of the Christian saint who
has suffered in the crucible of an incurable
disease. The crying over, the bargaining
done, the anger spilt, this one waits. While a
body grows weaker and weaker, a Christian
spirit unconquerable, victorious is being
delivered from the evil one!

Let us remember what Mr. Valiant-for-
truth in *The Pilgrim's Progress* says, as he
goes to God: "My sword I give to him that
shall succeed me in my pilgrimage, and my
courage and skill to him that can get it. My
marks and scars I carry with me, to be a witness for me that I have fought his battles
who will now be my rewarder. So he
passed over, and the trumpets sounded for
him on the other side."

11
The Signature

1 Chronicles 29:5-15

Our Father who art in heaven, Hallowed be thy name. Thy kingdom come, Thy will be done, On earth as it is in heaven. Give us this day our daily bread; And forgive us our debts, As we also have forgiven our debtors; And lead us not into temptation, But deliver us from evil (Matt. 6:9-13, RSV).

For thine is the kingdom, and the power, and the glory, for ever. Amen (v. 13b).

With these words we come to the end of the Lord's Prayer. Many scholars would say we came to the end of the prayer in the last chapter! For, indeed, the words above are not found in the oldest and best manuscripts. They were added, as I believe under the guidance of the Holy Spirit, by the early Christians. These words are a response, as it were, to the prayer. This response was added by second-generation Christians in a time of persecution, upheaval, and turmoil. These particular words were added to the prayer as an act of faith and perspective.

Thine is the kingdom, and the power, and the glory, for ever. These words were in the Bible of the early Christians, the Old Testament, in a very meaningful passage. David embodied their feelings in his words concerning the building of the Temple (1 Chron. 29). The king reminded his people that the house they were going to build was not just anybody's house; this was God's house, the symbol of his presence with the people and his glory among creation. They must never forget that it was through God's mercy and grace that they were even able to build the Temple.

The early Christians found in this ancient story of the building of the Temple a reflection of their own feelings. The church is God's creation, brought forth by his design and plan and intention. Its power, glory, and very life are a response to his gentle touch. So it was natural for the early Christians to pray the Lord's Prayer in corporate worship, realizing that they were part of each other. Together they composed the body of Christ. How significant it is that all the pronouns in the prayer are plural!

This prayer helped the early Christians focus upon who they were. Only one who was a disciple could pray these petitions. Only one who knelt at God's throne and sought his will, his purpose, and his people knew the meaning of the prayer. Through generations of Christians, for twenty centuries, the church has been praying together this prayer and including this last phrase. In good times and bad, in persecution and joy, still the cry echoes through this weary world: "Thine is the kingdom, and the power, and the glory, for ever"!

How important it is in our time to recover that sense of who we are as the church. In this twentieth century, churches are under pressure to be all things, to reflect prevailing moral standards and to flee unpopular godly stands. Our chief task is to remember who we are. If we can do that, we can then tell the world the church is God's church, the kingdom it represents is God's kingdom, the power promised it is God's power, and the end of all is God's glory.

But these added words are more than the church's fervent prayer for strength mixed with joyous response of commitment. There is personal application in the life of the individual Christian. No doubt in every worship service of the early church these words brought conviction to each worshiper. The grim picture rises of the Christian, having been healed, fed, led by God's grace daily to the fountain of forgiveness, now developing spiritual amnesia, becoming careless and ungrateful about spiritual things. There was then, and is now, the danger of the Christian assuming his is the power, the glory, and the kingdom. This was King David's fear concerning the building of the Temple. This fear led to the adding of this final phrase to the prayer as a reminder to individual Christians. Look more closely at the words of this final phrase.

Thine Is the Kingdom. We have seen the center of Jesus' preaching to be the kingdom of God. The nature of that kingdom is aptly pictured in the story of a poor and illiterate man who was converted by a street evangelist. He joined a little church nearby and was richly blessed in Christian fellowship and growth. But one night he came from church despondent. It seems the men of the church all wore red jerseys with a name on them. Neither the man nor his wife, both being unable to read, knew the jerseys represented the church ball team. The faithful wife resolved to mend the situation however. Not many days later, she presented her husband with a bright red jersey, with letters seen on a sign across the street sewn on it. With beaming face, the good man wore it to the next church meeting with great pride and more truth than he realized. His red jersey had these words emblazoned upon it: "Under New Management"!

God's kingdom is slowly, silently growing; suffering yet unconquerable and un-
ending. Beside it the kingdoms of this
world, whether structured and propped up
by Napoleon or Idi Amin, are but pale shadows and empty hulls. They are but gropings
in the dark, a further twisted slavery of an
already crippled and chained world. All our
kingdoms lay like empty shells upon the
shores of his kingdom.

> Come, O come, immortal Savior,
> Come and take thy royal throne;
> Come, and reign, and reign forever,
> Be the kingdom all thine own![1]

Thine Is the Power. Planted right in the
middle of this last phrase is an admission of
our lack of power. Are you able to com-
mand food from the soil? Can I lay claim to
bestow upon myself the riches of God's
forgiveness? Can even the strongest and
best among us deliver himself from the
power of the evil one? Of course not; yet
how easily and how soon we forget. These
words, *thine is the power,* are a public con-
fession both to ourselves and the person
next to us that we are powerless. We are
powerless to give real meaning to life. We
are like the Christmas toy, our lives come
without batteries, and we must find power
through God. We are powerless in the midst

of a world power-hungry and power-crazy. Again, like the advertisement of a toy, this world can be taken apart in less than a minute!

Yet we cannot even imagine the magnitude of God's power. What person, scientist or dictator can mold galaxies of space or even the tiny toes of a new baby? The puniness of human power is clear when we remember that just an average earthquake is a million times more powerful than the atomic bombs of World War II. A hurricane can generate more energy in ten seconds than our country uses in a year. And the run-of-the-mill lightning bolt could light your home for thirty-five years.

Our government pours millions of dollars into efforts to reform and rehabilitate people. In this area, we see God's power at its greatest. In raising Jesus from the dead and in raising you and me from our spiritual death and changing the deathward direction of our lives, the power of God is revealed in awesome power.

> Lord, now indeed I find
> Thy pow'r, and thine alone,
> Can change the leper's spots
> And melt the heart of stone.[2]

Thine Is the Glory. How ephemeral is the glory of earth. King Tut was laid away in

splendor so glorious that even to behold the
treasure brings forth gasps. But long ago,
grave robbers spit upon his honor, fame,
and respect. Charlemagne was called *the
Great* with good reason, and nations trem-
bled at his step. Yet in the midst of the Second World War, a soldier asked his superior
officer what to do with the great emperor's
bones: "We've got them in the back of the
jeep!" How ephemeral is earth's glory. Like
the gorgeous butterfly, the movie star or
music idol struts and frets and blasphemes
his tiny hour and is seen no more.

The Bible is majestic in its pictures of
God's everlasting glory:

The earth is the Lord's and the fulness thereof,/
the world and those who dwell therein;/for he
has founded it upon the seas,/and established it
upon the rivers./Lift up your heads, O gates!/and
be lifted up, O ancient doors!/that the King of
glory may come in./Who is the King of glory?/
The Lord, strong and mighty,/the Lord, mighty
in battle!/Lift up your heads, O gates!/and be
lifted up, O ancient doors!/that the King of glory
may come in!/Who is this King of glory?/The
Lord of hosts,/he is the King of glory! (Ps.
24:1-2,7-10).

The only *lasting* glory we can know and
experience is the reflection of God's glory in
the lives of his people. Archibald Rutledge
tells of an old tugboat which was used to

ferry folk across the Santee River. Rutledge says he hated to use the ferry because both the boat and its pilot were in such need of repair. The former needed painting, polishing, and scrubbing; the latter needed scrubbing, shaving, and clean clothes. But one day Rutledge approached the ferry landing to see a sight his eyes refused to accept! Here was the boat shining in a new coat of paint, with decks swabbed and brass polished. The pilot was clean-shaven and immaculate in a white uniform and kindly smile. To Rutledge's amazed inquiry, the pilot replied, "Cap'n, it is just this way: I got a glory!"[3]

Here is a reflection of the only lasting glory this world knows—the glory of God reflected in the heart of his people. It is a glory reflected through the ages in the worship of God's people. Seldom have I thrilled to the silent singing of the ages as I did standing in the ruins of beautiful Melrose Abbey in Scotland. To think that in these majestic ruins, a thousand years ago, a strong church reflected God's glory and grace!

Thine is the kingdom, and the power, and the glory, for ever. Amen. This is the signature of the early church. It is appropriate for you and me to sing the prayer both with this phrase and with our lives, as they did.

For our Lord is not merely king for a day, he is Lord of lords, King of kings—Forever, Amen!

Notes

1. B. B. McKinney, "Glorious Is Thy Name," *Baptist Hymnal* (Nashville: Broadman Press, 1975), No. 59.

2. Elvina M. Hall, "Jesus Paid It All," *Baptist Hymnal* (Nashville: Broadman Press, 1975), No. 156.

3. Archibald Rutledge. *It Will Be Daybreak Soon* (New York: Fleming H. Revell Company, 1939), pp. 28-30.